D0900634

THE NATURE AND MISSION OF THEOLOGY

JOSEPH CARDINAL RATZINGER

The Nature and Mission of Theology

Essays to Orient Theology in Today's Debates

TRANSLATED BY ADRIAN WALKER

IGNATIUS PRESS   SAN FRANCISCO

Title of the German original:
Wesen und Auftrag der Theologie:
Versuche zu ihrer Ortsbestimmung im Disput der Gegenwart
© 1993 Johannes Verlag, Einsiedeln

Cover art: Jesus announcing to the Apostles that he is soon to
leave them. Detail from the sarcophagus "The Apostles in Pain".
Bas-relief (4th century A.D.). Musee Lapidaire d'Art Chretien.
Scala/Art Resource, New York

Cover design by Roxanne Mei Lum

Contents

PART 3:
APPLICATIONS

Foreword

Theology and theologians have become a common and at the same time controversial topic of discussion in the Church, indeed, in Western society in general. If I am right, two things are expected of the theologian in the modern world. On the one hand, he is supposed to subject the traditions of Christianity to critical examination by the light of reason, to distill from them the essential core which can be appropriated for use today, and thereby also place the institutional Church within her proper limits. But at the same time he is also expected to respond to the need for religion and transcendence, a need which simply refuses to be ignored, by giving guiding orientations and meaningful content which can be responsibly accepted today. In the emerging world society an additional task devolves upon him: he must promote interreligious dialogue and contribute to the development of a planetary ethos whose key concepts are justice, peace and the integrity of creation. Finally, however, the theologian should also be a comforter of souls, who helps individuals to be reconciled with themselves and to overcome their alienations. In fact, the purely collective consolation of a better world of the future where universal peace reigns has proved to be thoroughly unsatisfying.

While the theologian is busily working to meet these expectations, the institutional Church often appears to be an annoying impediment. This is especially true of the Magisterium of the Catholic Church, which presupposes that Christianity, especially in its Catholic variety, has a determinate content and thus confronts our thinking with a prior given, which cannot be manipulated at will and which alone gives to the theologian's words their distinctive significance above and beyond all purely political or philosophical discourse. To do theology— as the Magisterium understands theology—it is not sufficient merely to calculate how much religion can reasonably be expected of man and to utilize bits and pieces of the Christian tradition accordingly. Theology is born when the arbitrary judgment of reason encounters a limit, in that we discover something which we have not excogitated ourselves but which has been revealed to us. For this reason, not every religious theory has the right to label itself as Christian or Catholic theology simply because it wishes to do so; whoever would lay claim to this title is obliged to accept as meaningful the prior given which goes along with it.

Everyone is free—within the framework of the responsibility of conscience before the truth—to think whatever this responsibility permits him to think or to say. But not everyone is free to assert that what he says represents Catholic theology. Here there is a sort of "trademark", a historical identity which the Magisterium knows it is called to defend. As the facts stand, however, what is really an effort to protect a historical (and, as we believe, God-given) identity is constantly construed as an attack upon intellectual freedom, all the more so as this identity is often a stumbling block for the contemporary mind, inasmuch as certain of its contents irritate our mentality and lifestyle. When the Magisterium takes exception to theologians who would liberate us from such irritations, it can even appear as a personal menace.

There is, to be sure, the other front as well: ordinary believers see in the work of present-day theologians a threat to all they hold sacred. The unrestricted application of scientific methods to matters of faith appears to be sheer presumption, whereby man oversteps his limits and undermines his own foundations. Certain sectors of the Church regard with growing suspicion the business of the theologians, who seem to be much too closely allied with the powers of the *Zeitgeist*.

In this situation, the dialogue concerning theology and the clarification of its methods, its mission and its limits have become urgent. The individual sections of this book were occasioned by the challenges of this dialogue. They do not form a systematic treatise on theology, a project which my professional obligations unfortunately do not permit me to undertake. Rather, the pieces assembled here represent so many preliminary approaches to the subject from diverse points of view. I hope that precisely in their openness to further development these first efforts can help the nature of the theologian's work in today's circumstances to be better understood as well as to sustain it in its essential task: to serve the knowledge of the truth of revelation and, in so doing, unity in the Church.

Rome
Feast of the Assumption of Mary, 1992

PART I

PRESUPPOSITIONS AND BASES
OF THEOLOGICAL WORK

Faith, Philosophy and Theology

1. The Unity of Philosophy and Theology in Early Christianity

At first glance, the question of the relationship between faith and philosophy seems to be quite abstract. But for Christians in the age of the nascent Church, it was not so: it was this question which made possible the first images of Christ, and we can even say that in its earliest beginnings Christian art arose out of the quest for the true philosophy. It was philosophy which enabled the first plastic expression of the faith. The most ancient Christian sculptures which have come down to us are found on sarcophagi of the third century. Their iconographical canon comprises three figures: the shepherd, the *orans* and the philosopher.[1] This association is significant, for it means that one of the roots of Christian art lies in the conquest of death. The three figures, in fact, are a response to the radical challenge which death poses to man. In this regard, the significance of the first two personages is immediately evident to us. Even though we must be circumspect about a straightforward christological and ecclesiological interpretation of the shepherd and of the *orans*, the fact remains that they contain an unmistakable reference to the foundations of Christian hope. There is the shepherd, who even in the midst of the valley of the shadow of death inspires a confidence capable of saying "I fear no evil" (Ps 23:4). There is the escort of prayer, which accompanies the soul on its pilgrimage and protects it. But what does the philosopher represent in this context? The depiction of the philosopher is modeled on the image of the Cynic, the itinerant preacher of philosophy. He is not

[1] Cf. F. Gerke, *Christus in der spätantiken Plastik*, 3d ed. (Mainz, 1948), 5; cf. in addition F. van der Meer, *Die Ursprünge christlicher Kunst* (Freiburg, 1982), 51ff.

moved by erudite theories: "He preaches because death is at his heels."[2] He does not seek hypotheses but to win possession of life by overcoming death. The Christian philosopher, as has been said, is portrayed according to this pattern, yet there is something different about him; he carries in his hand the Gospel, from which he learns, not words, but facts. He is the true philosopher, because he has knowledge of the mystery of death. Gerke sums up the vision of Christianity represented in this earliest Christian art in the following statement: "It is not the universe of the Bible and of sacred history which is the focal point of the most ancient Christian works of art but rather the philosopher, who is interpreted as the prototype of the *homo christianus* who has received the revelation of the true paradise through the Gospel."[3]

The fusion of Christianity and philosophy expressed here artistically in response to the question of death, which is seen as the only real existential question facing man, soon attains an even more concentrated density: the figure of the philosopher now becomes the image of Christ himself. The aim is not to picture how Christ looked but rather to portray who and what he was, namely, the perfect philosopher. Christ appears, as Gerke puts it beautifully, in the guise of the one who has summoned him.[4] Philosophy, the search for meaning in the face of death, is now represented as the search for Christ. In the resurrection of Lazarus, he stands forth as the one philosopher who gives an effectual answer by changing death and, therefore, changing life itself. In this way what had already been a conviction since the Apologists became a visible object of contemplation. As early as the second century, Justin Martyr had characterized Christianity as the true philosophy, for which he adduced two main reasons. First, the philosopher's essential task is to search for God. Second, the attitude

[2] Ibid., 6.
[3] Ibid., 7.
[4] Ibid., 8.

of the true philosopher is to live according to the Logos and in its company. Christian existence means life in conformity to the Logos; that is why Christians are the true philosophers and why Christianity is the true philosophy.[5] Such affirmations, which may have an abstract ring for us, could serve as clear illustrations of what it means to be a Christian because the itinerant philosopher was a familiar feature of the environment in which men lived. The experience of absurdity, the lack of orientation and the anguish which it spawned offered a lucrative market in which to make a living. This experience drew, as it does today, both counterfeiters of philosophy as well as men who had really been moved by the plight of others and were in a position to help. The philosopher thus furnished, despite all disappointments and falsifications which occurred in this marketplace, the imaginative form which made it possible to grasp the import of Christ and of the Resurrection.

Whoever lives in today's world with his eyes open knows that all of this does not belong simply to the past. The certainty about death and the path to life which Christianity had guaranteed for centuries has been deeply shaken on every side, and in the aftermath the number of the "wise" who would offer for sale the item "philosophy" is once again everywhere on the rise. This may be significant for our inquiry concerning the relationship between faith and philosophy insofar as it reminds professional philosophers and theologians that they are expected to provide something transcending all erudition, namely, an answer to the great questions of life, such as, what is human existence really about? or, what must we do to live our lives successfully? I think that we must not lose sight of this appeal as we pursue our investigation, because it contains an actual glimpse of the element which binds philosophy and

---

[5] Cf. O. Michel, φιλοσοφια in: *ThWNT* 9:185; important observations may also be found in H. U. von Balthasar, "Philosophie, Christentum, Mönchtum", in: idem, *Sponsa Verbi*, 2d ed. (Einsiedeln, 1971), 349–87 [H. U. von Balthasar, "Philosophy, Christianity, Monasticism", in: idem, *Spouse of the Word. Explorations in Theology II* (San Francisco, 1991), 333–72].

theology together. On the other hand, how the two disciplines are related in the concrete and how their distinct claims
to rationality can be safeguarded within their relationship are
questions which naturally cannot be adequately answered on
that basis alone; they require a methodical effort in their own
right.

2. From Distinction to Opposition

We have seen that in the early period of its history Christianity regarded itself as philosophy, indeed, as the philosophy par
excellence. Could we still affirm the same today? Or, if we
are not disposed to do so, why not? What has changed? How,
then, must we define their relationship correctly? The identification of Christianity and philosophy was indebted to a determinate conception of philosophy which gradually came under
criticism by Christian thinkers and was finally abandoned once
and for all in the thirteenth century. The distinction of the two
fields, which is above all the work of Saint Thomas Aquinas,
draws the lines of demarcation between them in roughly the
following manner. Philosophy is the search of unaided reason
for answers to the ultimate questions about reality. Philosophical knowledge comprises exclusively that sort of knowledge
which reason as such can gain by itself, without the guidance
of revelation. It thus derives its certainty from argument alone,
and its assertions are worth precisely as much as the arguments
which support them. Theology, in contrast, is rational reflection upon God's revelation; it is faith seeking understanding. It
does not, therefore, discover its contents by itself but rather receives them from revelation, in order then to understand them
in their inner coherence and intelligibility. With a terminology
still inchoate in Saint Thomas' works, the domains of inquiry
belonging to philosophy and theology were distinguished, re-
spectively, as the natural and supernatural orders. These dis-
tinctions reached their full rigor only in the modern period,
which then read them back into Saint Thomas, thus imposing

on him an interpretation which severs him more radically from the preceding tradition than is warranted by the texts alone.[6]

Such historical questions, however, need not occupy us here. It is at all events a fact that, since the late Middle Ages, philosophy has been paired with pure reason while theology has been coupled with faith and that this distinction has molded the image of the one as well as of the other. But once this process of separation is complete, the question inevitably arises: Can philosophy and theology still enter into any kind of mutual relationship at the level of methodology? Meanwhile, this possibility is contested by both sides with weighty arguments. As an example of the denial coming from the philosophical camp, I cite only Heidegger and Jaspers. For Heidegger, philosophy is by nature questioning. Whoever believes he has the answer already is no longer capable of philosophizing. Since the philosophical question is folly in the eyes of theology, Christian philosophy is a sham. Jaspers shares the opinion that he who supposes himself in possession of the answer has failed as a philosopher: the open movement of transcendence is interrupted in favor of an imagined ultimate certainty.[7] It must be granted, in fact, that if a reason entirely neutral vis-à-vis the Christian faith is part and parcel of the philosophical act, and if philosophical knowledge necessarily excludes any prior given which streams into thinking from faith, then the philosophical activity of a believing Christian must indeed appear to be something of a fiction. But are the answers of the Christian faith really such as to cut off the path of thought? Is it not the

---

[6] For a survey of the historical issues, see F. van Steenberghen, *Die Philosophie im 13. Jahrhundert* (Munich/Paderborn, 1977); É. Gilson, *Le Thomisme*, 5th ed. (Paris, 1945) [É. Gilson, *The Christian Philosophy of St. Thomas* (New York, 1950)]; A. Hayen, *Thomas von Aquin gestern und heute* (Frankfurt, 1953); for a systematic examination of the same subject, see É. Gilson, *Der Geist der mittelalterlichen Philosophie* (Vienna, 1950) [É. Gilson, *The Spirit of Medieval Philosophy* (London, 1950)].

[7] Cf. J. Pieper, *Verteidigungsrede für die Philosophie* (Munich, 1966), 128; W. M. Neidl, *Christliche Philosophie—eine Absurdität?* (Salzburg, 1981).

case that answers concerning ultimate reality by nature always open into that which has not been expressed and perhaps cannot be expressed? Might it not be that it is only such answers that give questions their true depth and drama? Could it not be that they radicalize not only questioning but thinking itself, setting it on its path instead of obstructing it? Jaspers himself once remarked that thought which severs itself from the great tradition falls into a seriousness which is progressively emptied of content.[8] Does this not suggest that familiarity with a great answer such as that conveyed by faith stimulates rather than obstructs authentic questioning?

We shall have to return to these considerations. Before we do, it is necessary to shift vantage points for a moment in order to examine the rejection of philosophy from the side of theology. Opposition to philosophy as the alleged corrupter of theology is very ancient. It can already be found in Tertullian, who expressed it with bitter acrimony, but it flamed up again and again in the Middle Ages and attained a remarkable radicality in the later work of Saint Bonaventure, to cite one example.[9] Martin Luther inaugurated a new era of antagonism to philosophy for the sake of the unadulterated Word of God. His battle cry, "*sola scriptura*", was a declaration of war not merely against the classical interpretation of Scripture advanced by tradition and the Magisterium of the Church but also against Scholasticism, that is, the use of Aristotle and Plato in theology. For Luther, the incorporation of philosophy into theology automatically destroys the message of grace, hence, the gospel itself in its very

[8] K. Jaspers and R. Bultmann, *Die Frage der Entmythologisierung* (Munich, 1954), 12 [K. Jaspers and R. Bultmann, *Myth and Christianity: An Inquiry into the Possibility of Religion without Myth* (New York: The Noonday Press, 1960)]; cf. J. Pieper, *Über die Schwierigkeit heute zu glauben: Aufsätze und Reden* (Munich, 1974), 302 [J. Pieper, *Problems of Modern Faith: Essays and Addresses* (Chicago, 1985)].

[9] Cf. J. Ratzinger, *Die Geschichtstheologie des heiligen Bonaventura* (Munich/Zürich, 1959), 140–61 [J. Ratzinger, *The Theology of History in St. Bonaventure* (Chicago, 1989)].

heart. In fact, in his view philosophy is the self-expression of man who in ignorance of grace attempts to construct for himself his own wisdom and righteousness. The antithesis between righteousness based on works and righteousness through grace, which according to Luther represents the line of demarcation between Christ and the Antichrist, thus becomes in his eyes identical to the antithesis between philosophy and a reflection inspired by the biblical word. On this reading, philosophy is the sheer corruption of theology.[10] It is well known that in our century Karl Barth sharpened this protest against the presence of philosophy in theology with his contestation of the *analogia entis*, which he considered an invention of the Antichrist and the only, though insuperable, obstacle to his becoming a Catholic. It must be remembered that the catchword *analogia entis* is simply a term for the ontological option of Catholic theology, for its synthesis of the philosophical idea of being and the biblical conception of God. Against this continuity between philosophy's search for the ultimate causes and theology's appropriation of biblical faith, Barth sets a radical discontinuity. Faith, according to Barth, unmasks all of reason's images of God as idols. It does not draw its life from synthesis but from paradox. It receives the wholly other God, whom our thinking can neither produce nor call into question.[11]

The way thus seems to be barred on either side. On the one hand, philosophy defends itself against the prior given which faith implies for thinking; it feels that such a given inhibits the purity and freedom of its reflection. Theology, on the other hand, defends itself against the prior given of philosophical knowledge as a threat to the purity and novelty of faith. In re-

[10] Cf. B. Lohse, *Martin Luther: Eine Einführung in sein Leben und sein Werk* (Munich, 1981), 166ff. [B. Lohse, *Martin Luther: An Introduction to His Life and Work* (Philadelphia, 1986)].

[11] On the evolution of Barth's thought concerning the *analogia entis*, see in particular H. U. von Balthasar, *Karl Barth*, 4th ed. (Einsiedeln, 1976) [H. U. von Balthasar, *The Theology of Karl Barth: Exposition and Interpretation* (San Francisco, 1992)].

ality, however, the pathos of such denials cannot be maintained to the end. How could philosophical thinking make a beginning at all without prior givens? Since Plato, philosophy has always thrived on critical dialogue with some great religious tradition. Its own standing has always been bound to the status of the traditions which lie at the starting point of its struggle for truth. Whenever it discontinues such dialogue, it quickly dies out even as pure philosophy. Conversely, in reflecting upon the revealed Word, theology simply cannot avoid proceeding in a philosophical manner. As soon as it no longer repeats, no longer merely gathers historical marginalia, but endeavors to understand in the proper sense of the word, it enters into the realm of philosophical thinking. As a matter of fact, neither Luther nor Barth managed to divest himself of philosophical thinking and of a certain philosophical patrimony, and the very least that can be said is that the history of Evangelical theology is no less profoundly shaped by exchange with philosophy than that of its Catholic counterpart.

At this point, however, it is necessary to draw a distinction, the analysis of which will also lead us directly to the heart of our problem. The refusal which in manifold variations remains a constant theme from Luther to Barth does not, on closer examination, regard philosophy as such but rather metaphysics as envisaged by Plato and Aristotle. Even Luther's antimetaphysical posture is directed primarily against the late medieval Scholasticism with which he was familiar; it is kept within bounds by his adherence to the dogma of the early Church. Thanks to its faithfulness to the ancient Creeds, Protestant orthodoxy, which built up its own version of Scholasticism, acted as a further check to the revolutionary element in Luther's position, which thus achieved its full breakthrough only in the second half of the modern period, when the dogma of the ancient Church itself appears as the epitome of the hellenization and ontologization of faith. It is a fact that both the doctrine of the triune God and the profession of faith in Christ as true God and true man had moved the ontological content of the Bible's utterances to the center of Christian thought and belief. The critique of hellenization which has dominated the theological scene since the nineteenth century sees in that shift a defection from the pure faith in salvation taught by the Bible. The actual motive force behind this judgment is the rejection of metaphysics, whereas, at the very same time, the doors are thrown open to experiments in historically focused philosophy. One may well say that these developments in theology have been among the principal influences at work in the progressive replacement of metaphysics by history which has taken place in philosophy since Kant, while the evolution thus set in motion in philosophy has in turn had a powerful countereffect upon options in theology.[12] The resulting situation of philosophy is such that for many the only reasonable course, even from the philosophical point of view, is to disavow, or at least to forgo, ontology. However, it is not possible to stop with the renunciation of ontology: in the long run, the concept of God itself follows in its wake. It then becomes logical, perhaps the only solution still possible, to interpret faith as pure paradox, as Barth does, at least in his initial phase. But this gamble also fails to restore faith's original accord with reason. Faith which turns into paradox thus loses its capacity to explain and penetrate everyday life. On the other hand—it is impossible to live in pure contradiction. To my mind, this is sufficient proof that no one can exclude the question of metaphysics from philosophical inquiry, degrading it to a holdover from Hellenism. To cease asking about the origin and goal of the whole of reality is to leave out the characteristic element of philosophical questioning itself. Although the past and present opposition to the use of philosophy in theology is aimed for the most part at metaphysics alone and does not intend to eliminate philosophy altogether, the theologian stands to lose most by divorcing the

---

[12] On this point, see H. Thielicke, *Glauben und Denken in der Neuzeit* (Tübingen, 1983); also instructive is U. Asendorf, *Luther und Hegel. Untersuchungen zur Grundlegung einer neuen systematischen Theologie* (Wiesbaden, 1982).

two. For his part, a philosopher who really gets to the bottom of things can never rid himself of the goad of the question of God, which is the question regarding the origin and goal of being as such.

3. Toward a New Relationship

In the foregoing, we began by giving a rough sketch of the distinction between philosophy and theology. While we did so, it became apparent that in the history of the two disciplines this distinction has increasingly tended to take the form of an antithesis. It also became clear, however, that the development of an opposition between philosophy and theology has itself transformed the two sciences. In the wake of this evolution, philosophy tends more and more to cast off ontology, that is, its own primordial question, while theology discards the fundamental principles which originally made it possible, in its characteristic double tension between revelation and reason. In contrast, we affirmed that philosophy as such cannot do without ontology and that theology is no less obliged to have recourse to it. The exclusion of ontology from theology does not emancipate philosophical thinking but paralyzes it. The extinction of ontology in the sphere of philosophy, far from purifying theology, actually deprives it of its solid basis. Contrary to the common hostility toward ontology, which is apparently becoming the sole link between contemporary philosophers and theologians, we held that both disciplines need this dimension of thought and that it is here that they find themselves indissolubly associated.

We must now render this general diagnosis somewhat more precise and concrete. After having thoroughly investigated the aporia of the antithesis, we must frame the question positively: In what sense does faith need philosophy? In what way is philosophy open to faith and oriented from within toward dialogue with its message? I would like to sketch very briefly three levels of an answer to these queries.

a. We have already encountered a first level of correlation between philosophical and theological inquiry in our glance at the earliest images of faith: both faith and philosophy confront the primordial question which death addresses to man. Now, the question of death is only the radical form of the question about how to live rightly. It asks whence man comes and whither he is going. It seeks an origin and a destination. Death, the one question which it is impossible to ignore forever, is thus a metaphysical thorn lodged in man's being. Man has no choice but to ask what might be the meaning of this final limit. On the other hand, it is clear to every thinking person that only someone with firsthand knowledge of what lies beyond death could give a well-founded answer to that question. In consequence, if faith knows that such an answer has in fact been given, it demands the attention and joint reflection which are the special activities of questioning inquiry. Such an answer by no means causes the shipwreck of inquiry, as Jaspers opines. On the contrary, questioning founders when there is no hope of finding an answer. Faith hears the answer because it keeps the question alive. It can receive the answer as such only if it is able to understand its relevance to the question. When faith speaks of the resurrection of the dead, what is at stake is not a more or less abstruse assertion about an unverifiable future place and an unknown future time but the comprehension of man's being within the whole of reality. The fundamental problem of justice is therefore also in play, and this is inseparable from the problem of hope. The central concern is the relationship between history and ethos, between human action and the unmanipulable character of reality. The sort of questions involved here, which, though formulated diversely from period to period, remain essentially the same, can mark progress only in the exchange between question and answer, philosophical and theological reflection. This dialogue of human thought with the prior givens of faith will have one aspect when it is conducted in strictly philosophical terms and another when it is expressly theological. But both kinds of dialogue must maintain a mutual relationship, and neither can wholly dispense with the other.

b. We have likewise already alluded to the second level of correlation in the preceding reflections: faith advances a philosophical, more precisely, an ontological claim when it professes the existence of God, indeed, of a God who has power over reality as a whole. A powerless God is, in fact, a contradiction in terms. If he cannot act, cannot speak and be spoken to, he may be considered the concluding hypothesis of the reasoning process but has nothing to do with what the religious belief of mankind means by "God". The scope of the assertion that there is a God who is the creator and savior of the whole universe reaches beyond the religious community which makes it. It is not intended as a symbolic representation of the unnameable, which looks one way in this religion and another in that, but as a statement about reality as it is in itself. This breakthrough in thinking about God to a fundamental claim on human reason as such is wholly evident in the religious critique of the prophets and the biblical wisdom literature. If the prophets ridicule man-made idols with mordant acerbity and set the only real God in contrast to them, in the wisdom books the same spiritual movement is at work as among the pre-Socratics at the time of the early Greek enlightenment. To the extent that the prophets see in the God of Israel the primordial creative ground of all reality, it is quite clear that what is taking place is a religious critique for the sake of a correct understanding of this reality itself. Here the faith of Israel unquestionably steps beyond the limits of a single people's peculiar worship: it puts forth a universal claim, whose universality has to do with its being rational. Without the prophetic religious critique, the universalism of Christianity would have been unthinkable. It was this critique which, in the very heart of Israel itself, prepared that synthesis of Hellas and the Bible which the Fathers labored to achieve. For this reason, it is incorrect to reduce the concepts *logos* and *aletheia*, upon which John's Gospel centers the Christian message, to a strictly Hebraic interpretation, as if *logos* meant "word" merely in the sense of God's speech in history, and *aletheia* signified nothing more than "trustworthiness" or "fidelity". For the very same reason, there is no basis for the opposite accusation that John distorted biblical thought in the direction of Hellenism. On the contrary, he stands in the classical sapiential tradition. It is precisely in John's writings that one can study, both in its origins and in its outcome, the inner movement of biblical faith in God and biblical Christology toward philosophical inquiry.[13]

Is the world to be understood as originating from a creative intellect or as arising out of a combination of probabilities in the realm of the absurd? Today as yesterday, this alternative is the decisive question for our comprehension of reality; it cannot be dodged. Whoever, on the other hand, would draw faith back into paradox or into a pure historical symbolism fails to perceive its unique historical position, whose defense engaged both the prophets and the apostles in equal measure. The universality of faith, which is a basic presupposition of the missionary task, is both meaningful and morally defensible only if this faith really is oriented beyond the symbolism of the religions toward an answer meant for all, an answer which also appeals to the common reason of mankind. The exclusion of this common appeal inevitably puts an end to any communication to men which touches upon ultimate realities. The question of God, therefore, obliges theology to take a position in the philosophical debate. When it gives up the claim to the reasonability of its fundamental assertions, it does not return to a purer attitude of belief but rather betrays a fundamental element of its own constitution. By the same token, a philosophy which wishes to remain true to its object must open itself to faith's claim on reason. The coordination of philosophy and theology is indispensable on this second level as well.

---

[13] Important observations on these questions are offered by H. Gese, "Der Johannesprolog", in idem, *Zur biblischen Theologie* (Munich, 1977), 155–201.

c. Finally, I would like to suggest a few remarks on the controversy which this issue aroused in medieval theology. In the works of Bonaventure there are two principal answers to the question whether and why it is legitimate to attempt a comprehension of the biblical message using methods of philosophical reasoning. The first answer relies on a statement from 1 Peter 3:15, which in the Middle Ages was the *locus classicus* for the justification of systematic theology in general: "Always be prepared to make a defense to anyone who calls you to account for the hope that is in you."[14] The Greek text is by far more expressive than any translation. Believers are enjoined to give an *apo-logia* regarding the *logos* of our hope to whoever asks for it. The *logos* must be so intimately their own that it can become *apo-logia*; through the mediation of Christians, the Word [*Wort*] becomes response [*Antwort*] to man's questions. At first glance, this seems to be a justification of theology purely for its apologetical value: one must be able to explain before others why one believes. This point is quite significant in its own right. Faith is not pure private decision, which as such does not really concern anyone else. It will and can show its credentials. It wishes to make itself understandable to others. It lays claim to being a *logos* and, therefore, to the never-failing capacity to become apo-logy. But at a deeper level, this apologetic interpretation of theology is a missionary one, and the missionary conception, in its turn, brings to light the inner nature of faith. Faith has the right to be missionary only if it truly transcends all traditions and constitutes an appeal to reason and an orientation toward the truth itself. However, if man is made to know reality and has to conduct his life, not merely as tradition dictates, but in conformity to the truth, faith also has the positive duty to be missionary. With its missionary claim, the Christian faith sets itself apart from the other religions which have appeared in history; this claim is implicit in its philosophical critique of the religions and can be justified only on that

[14] Bonaventura, *Sent.*, proœm. q 2 sed contra 1.

basis. The fact that today missionary dynamism threatens to trickle away into nothing goes hand in hand with the deficit in philosophy which characterizes the contemporary theological scene.

But we can identify another justification of theology in Bonaventure's work; though it seems at first to point in an entirely different direction, its inner tendency is to merge with what has been said so far. The Saint is aware that the citizenship of philosophy in theology is a contested issue. He concedes that there is a violence of reason which cannot be brought into harmony with faith. Nevertheless, he affirms that there is also an inquiry inspired by another motive. Faith can wish to understand because it is moved by love for the One upon whom it has bestowed its consent.[15] Love seeks understanding. It wishes to know ever better the one whom it loves. It "seeks his face", as Augustine never tires of repeating.[16] Love is the desire for intimate knowledge, so that the quest for intelligence can even be an inner requirement of love. Put another way, there is a coherence of love and truth which has important consequences for theology and philosophy. Christian faith can say of itself, I have found love. Yet love for Christ and of one's neighbor for Christ's sake can enjoy stability and consistency only if its deepest motivation is love for the truth. This adds a new aspect to the missionary element: real love of neighbor also desires to give him the deepest thing man needs, namely, knowledge and truth. In the first part we took as our starting point the problem of death considered as the philosophical thorn in the side of faith. We then discovered in the second part that the God question, together with its universal claim, is the place of philosophy in theology. We can now add a third element: love, the center of Christian reality on which "depend the law and the prophets", is at the same time eros for truth, and only so does it remain sound as agape for God and man.

[15] Ibid., q 2 ad 6.
[16] See, for example, *En in ps 104*, 3 C Chr XL p. 1537.

A Concluding Observation:
Gnosis, Philosophy and Theology

To conclude, I would like to return once more to the beginning, to the idea of the early Fathers that Christianity itself is
true philosophy. Otto Michel has pointed out that the Gnostics
avoided the word "philosophy". With the term "gnosis", they
expressed an even loftier claim. Philosophy, which always remains a question and awaits an answer which it cannot give on
its own, was too little for them. They pretended to possess clear
knowledge—knowledge in the sense of power to master the
world both on this side of death and beyond it.[17] Gnosis turns
out to be the negation of philosophy, whereas faith defends
both the grandeur and misery of philosophy. Are we not witnessing something quite similar today? Authentic philosophy,
with its ultimate uncertainty, disgusts us. We want, not philosophy, but gnosis, that is, exact, verifiable knowledge. Moreover, philosophy is to a great extent weary of itself. It shares the
impatience to become like the other academic disciplines both
in nature and in worth. It wishes to be just as "exact" as they
are. Yet it purchases exactitude at the price of its greatness, for
in so doing it is no longer able to pose those questions which
are proper to it alone. In becoming "exact", it joins the other
disciplines in taking, no longer the whole, but the particular as
its object. Nevertheless, man must not begin to be silent about
what we cannot speak of, for we thereby silence the characteristic dimension of our being.[18] Where exactness is raised to a

---

[17] Cf. on this point Michel, 185, n. 136.

[18] I am alluding here to the concluding sentence of L. Wittgenstein's *Trac-
tatus Logico-Philosophicus*, German-English (London/New York, 1961): "What
we cannot speak about we must consign to silence" (6.54). When Wittgenstein points to the inexpressible (6.522), he is doubtless in consonance with
the best philosophical, theological and mystical tradition; Wittgenstein likewise places himself within the mystical tradition when he characterizes philosophical propositions as the ladder which one must kick away when one "has

value so absolute that there is no further room for questioning beyond exact "gnosis", man loses his very self, for the questions belonging to man as such are taken away from him. Josef Pieper once remarked in a vision bordering on the apocalyptic that, "[I]t could very well happen that at the end of history the root of all things and the ultimate threat to existence—which, in fact, means the specific object of philosophical activity— can still be perceived only by those who believe."[19] Pieper's intention in this passage was not to describe the present state of things, to which such an assertion could doubtless not be applied. Nevertheless, though it looks forward to a possible future, this statement brings before our eyes an aspect of the whole situation which binds us today once more to the Fathers: faith does not menace philosophy but rather defends it against the total claim of gnosis. It defends philosophy because it needs it; faith needs philosophy because it needs man who questions and seeks. It is not questioning, in fact, which places obstacles to faith but that closure which no longer wants to question and holds truth to be unreachable or not worth striving for. Faith does not destroy philosophy, it champions it. Only when it takes up the cause of philosophy does it remain true to itself.

---

used them—as steps—to climb up beyond them" (6.54). But at the very moment he says this, the rejection of metaphysics and its total removal into the ineffable, which he seems to demand in 6.53, already stands refuted. In fact, in order for propositions to serve as a ladder for climbing beyond what can be said, they must themselves be steps in that direction. Otherwise, all that remains is what Wittgenstein enlarges on at the beginning of 6.53: "The correct method in philosophy would really be the following: to say nothing except what can be said, i.e., propositions of natural science." The "would really" shows that not even Wittgenstein regards this as the correct method.

[19] Pieper, *Über die Schwierigkeit heute zu glauben*, 303.

On the Essence of the
Academy and Its Freedom

The word "academic" arouses conflicting feelings today. It immediately connotes something out of date, a theory which has installed itself comfortably in a world of its own, where it can reflect without having to face the demands of reality. Perhaps people also recall that Plato was the creator of the academy; nevertheless, despite all the rehabilitations of Plato taking place in physical science and in other disciplines, such as political philosophy,[1] many regard Platonism as a flight into an unreal universe of pure ideas, as the epitome of an obsolete intellectual orientation. In one sphere only has the luster of the word "academic" remained untarnished, or even increased: where "academic freedom" is at issue. In a society which on the whole is shaped by the cry for freedom, but which, at the same time, is hedged round by constraints quite unimaginable in a pretechnological world, it has become vitally important that the mind have a haven of freedom which observes none but its own rules and is not subject to any set of norms issued by an outside authority. Talk of "academic freedom" is meant to erect a dam against the all-encompassing power of the bureaucracies as well as against the pressure emanating from the dictatorship of needs. The battle which is waged on this front admits of many variations. In the first place, it is a matter of defending the "useless disciplines"—the so-called "liberal arts"—against the predominance of utility. But the natural sciences also fight for the freedom to choose their object for themselves rather than have it prescribed to them by the demands of the market. Finally, there is the particular cry of theologians for their aca-

[1] Cf. J. Monod, *Zufall und Notwendigkeit. Philosophische Fragen der modernen Biologie*, 5th ed. (Munich, 1973; Paris, 1970); see especially 127ff.; 186 and passim.

demic freedom in relation to the institutional Church, their insistent demand for the right to make decisions regarding their inquiry and conclusions with as much independence as, for example, philosophers. It is thus well worth the effort to attempt a fundamental reflection on the original nature of the "academic".

How ought we to approach such questions? Do we not find that the individual forms of the academic are much too various to have anything like a common basis or to permit answers applicable to all of them in common? There is no denying the vast compass of what has to be included for consideration in the contemporary discussion of academic freedom. On the other hand, there must be some sort of common ground if the word "academic", which in this context serves to justify the claim to a specific sort of freedom, is to retain any meaning at all. However widely its particular realizations may diverge, all of them ultimately turn upon that fundamental birthright of the mind for independent inquiry and direction which was first formulated by Plato. Without immediately giving all too practical answers, I would like, therefore, to attempt to delineate a few essential properties of what, throughout all of its historical transformations, may be considered the enduring essence of the academic.[2]

1. Dialogue

Let us begin with a fact which, though situated close to the surface of the matter, is more than an external detail. The academy, as Plato conceived it, is first and foremost a place of dialogue. But what does the word "dialogue" really mean? After all, *dialogue* does not take place simply because people are talking. Mere talk is the deterioration of dialogue that occurs when there has been a failure to reach it. Dialogue first comes into

[2] The following considerations are very much indebted to the little book of J. Pieper, *Was heißt akademisch?*, 2d ed. (Munich, 1964); see also R. Guardini, *Verantwortung: Gedanken zur jüdischen Frage* (Munich, 1952).

being where there is not only speech but also listening. Moreover, such listening must be the medium of an encounter; this encounter is the condition of an inner contact which leads to mutual comprehension. Reciprocal understanding, finally, deepens and transforms the being of the interlocutors. Having enumerated the single elements of this transaction, let us now attempt to grasp the significance of each in turn.

The first element is listening. What takes place here is an event of opening, of becoming open to the reality of other things and people. We need to realize what an art it is to be able to listen attentively. Listening is not a skill, like working a machine, but a capacity simply to be which puts in requisition the whole person. To listen means to know and to acknowledge another and to allow him to step into the realm of one's own "I". It is readiness to assimilate his word, and therein his being, into one's own reality as well as to assimilate oneself to him in corresponding fashion. Thus, after the act of listening, I am another man, my own being is enriched and deepened because it is united with the being of the other and, through it, with the being of the world.

All of this presupposes that what my dialogue partner has to say does not concern merely some object falling within the range of empirical knowledge and of technical skills, that is, of external know-how. When we speak of dialogue in the proper sense, what we mean is an utterance wherein something of being itself, indeed, the person himself, becomes speech. This does not merely add to the mass of items of knowledge acquired and of performances registered but touches the very being of man as such, purifying and intensifying his potency to be who he is.

But a further dimension of dialogue, which pertains both to listening and to speaking, thus discloses itself. This is an element upon which the early Augustine set particular value. In fact, we can easily trace the story of Augustine's conversion in the records of his dialogues with his friends, in which the little academy of Cassiciacum groped its way toward the hour when a new word, which had been unknown to Plato, could at last tumble into its midst and become the beginning of a new life. Analyzing these colloquies in retrospect, Augustine concludes that the community of friends was capable of mutual listening and understanding because all of them together heeded the interior master, the truth.[3] Men are capable of reciprocal comprehension because, far from being wholly separate islands of being, they communicate in the same truth. The greater their inner contact with the one reality which unites them, namely, the truth, the greater their capacity to meet on common ground. Dialogue without this interior obedient listening to the truth would be nothing more than a discussion among the deaf.

Here we come upon a circumstance which, aside from its extraordinary importance in today's debate, at the same time reveals the perils to which dialogue is exposed. The capacity to reach a consensus presupposes the existence of a truth common to all. Consensus, however, must not try to pass itself off as a substitute for the truth. Let us stop at this point, which has led us right to the heart of the matter, in order to reflect upon a second characteristic of the "academic".

2. Freedom

From the very beginning, freedom has belonged to the essence of the academy and of its search for understanding. In this context, freedom means essentially two things. In the first place, it is the possibility to think everything, ask everything and say everything which appears worthy of being thought, asked and said in the effort to find the truth.[4] So far, we are quite

---

[3] On the philosophy of the early Augustine, see, for example, E. König, *Augustinus philosophus. Christlicher Glaube und philosophisches Denken in den Frühschriften Augustinus* (Munich, 1970).

[4] In relation to this section, see J. Ratzinger, "Freiheit und Bindung in

obviously within the range of what everyone today accepts and defends, at least in theory. Nonetheless, the question imposes itself: What justifies this freedom, which under certain circumstances can be so dangerous? What is its basis? What do we take this risk for? The answer, at least the only satisfying one, is that the truth itself, the truth for its own sake, is so precious that it warrants such a risk; otherwise, no one could dare to undertake it. However, we thereby immediately find ourselves in a dramatic conflict with all strategies of change and, at the same time, at the heart of the question concerning the foundation of our society in general. Let us attempt, therefore, to describe this point as precisely as possible. Josef Pieper defines it in the following manner: "The distinctive feature [of the academic] is above all this freedom from the necessity of pursuing some profit aim—this is authentic 'academic freedom', which, accordingly, is *per definitionem* wiped out as soon as the academic disciplines become mere technicians pursuing the objectives of some power interest of whatever sort."[5] "You can certainly believe that you have taken philosophy into your service; but behold, what has been taken into service is not philosophy."[6]

The question of freedom is inseparably linked to the question of truth. When truth is not a value in itself which merits both active interest and the expenditure of time independently of its results, profit can be the only criterion with which to evaluate knowledge. If this is the case, knowledge has its raison d'être no longer in itself but in the objectives which it serves. It then belongs to the domain of ends and means. In other words, in one form or another it is subordinate to power and its acquisition. We can put it in yet another way: if man were absolutely incapable of knowing the truth itself but only the

---

der Kirche", in: idem, *Kirche—Ökumene—Politik* (Einsiedeln, 1987), 165–82 [J. Ratzinger, "Freedom and Constraint in the Church" in: idem, *Church, Ecumenism and Politics: New Essays in Ecclesiology* (Slough, 1988), 182–203].

[5] Pieper, 28.

[6] Ibid., 29.

fitness for use which things have in view of particular aims, use and consumption would become the measure of all action and thought. In consequence, the world would no longer be anything but "material for praxis". We are thus in a position to see clearly the inexorable and ineluctable fundamental alternative, which to an ever greater extent has become *the* dilemma of the modern age, so that today it poses itself as the question upon which the whole destiny of our epoch hinges: Is truth accessible to man at all? Is the search for it worthwhile? Can we even say that the quest for truth and the knowledge that the truth is the lawful mistress of man are perhaps our only hope of salvation? Or is the final adieu to the whole business of truth, which emerges clearly in Francis Bacon's new logic, man's true liberation, which awakens him from his speculative reverie and allows him at last to take in his own hands the dominion over reality, in order to become "master and lord of nature"?[7] Which is right: Giambattista Vico's definition, according to which truth is exclusively what has been produced (and therefore what can be produced), or the Christian option that truth is prior to making?[8] The freedom which derives from Bacon's new thinking is the freedom to produce everything and to acknowledge no other lawfulness save man's capacity to do. Such freedom had certainly not been recognized previously and could set itself up as the true liberation, like the younger son, who takes possession of his own inheritance and sets out with it into the unknown. But the freedom to produce everything, which no longer perceives any obligation in the truth—

[7] In his *Novum Organum*, Francis Bacon attempted to redefine the nature of philosophy. It inquires no longer simply in order to find the truth but to acquire know-how, to achieve man's dominion over the world. Its aim is to achieve mastery over nature. Cf. Pieper, 20. The significance of Bacon in the spiritual revolution of the modern era is vigorously set forth by M. Kriele, *Befreiung und politische Aufklärung* (Freiburg, 1980), 78–82; in addition, see R. Spaemann and R. Löw, *Die Frage Wozu?* (Munich/Zürich, 1981), 100f.

[8] See J. Ratzinger, *Einführung in das Christentum* (Munich, 1968), 33–43 [J. Ratzinger, *Introduction to Christianity* (San Francisco, 1990), 30–39].

the father—is subject to the constraint that from now on using and being used alone hold sway over man. When all is said and done, therefore, it is a slave's freedom—even though it reveals its true nature only late in the game and even though it takes a long time before it has so ruined itself by bad management that it lands among the pigs' husks and must still envy the swine because they are not cursed with freedom. The most advanced outposts of modern spiritual evolution have already reached this point. On the other hand, the ecological outcry against man as the destroyer of nature is no solution as long as it does not include a renewal of the quest for the truth. "The truth shall make you free" (Jn 8:32)—today we are ready for a completely fresh appreciation of the immeasurable claim and the power of this saying of the Lord. The real choice of our time has become that between the freedom of production and the freedom of the truth. But the freedom to produce, unchecked by truth, means the dictatorship of ends in a world devoid of truth and thus enslaves man while appearing to set him free. Only when truth has value in itself and a glimpse of it outweighs every success, only then are we free; and this is why the only authentic freedom is the freedom of the truth.

3. The Center: Truth as the Basis and Measure of Freedom

This brings us to the truly decisive point of our reflections: "academic" freedom is freedom for the *truth*, and its justification is simply to exist for the sake of the truth, without having to look back toward the objectives it has reached. As she directs her gaze backward, Lot's wife is turned into a pillar of salt; Orpheus, climbing up to the light, lost everything when he glanced backward to assure himself of his success.[9]

Let us now make the attempt to express the idea itself as precisely as possible, in order to see as clearly as we can both

---

[9] This image is to be found in Pieper, 69, who borrows it from K. Weiß.

the claim and the consequences which it entails. It seems to me a significant fact that Romano Guardini, with his characteristic perspicacity and uncompromising honesty, formulated this idea in connection with the Jewish question. This is no accident, for then, in the darkest days of the Third Reich, the deadliness of the alliance of reason, the machine and politics had become fully manifest. What reason becomes when practical aims and the power of technique have been made the only god was by then plain for all to see; so too was the fact that only the continued authority of the truth, only its inviolability offered hope of salvation. What Guardini said at that time concerning the university remains a valid manifesto of the authentically academic spirit: "If the university has a spiritual significance, it is to be the place of inquiry after the truth, for truth alone—not for an ulterior end, but for its own sake: simply because it is truth."[10] Bishop Hermann Dietzfelbinger, on the occasion of his acceptance of the Romano Guardini Prize, expressed the same thought in relation to present-day concerns. In the course of his speech, he pointed out that a shift has taken place from the question of truth to the question of value and went on to recall that the ideas of nascent National Socialism had managed to legitimate themselves under the guise of constructive and liberating "values". The statement of Carl Friedrich von Weizsäcker which the Bishop cited in his speech deserves to be repeated here: "I maintain that in the long run only a truth-oriented society, not a happiness-oriented society, can succeed."[11]

However, if we bear in mind the context of the above-mentioned saying of Guardini, this means that the most effective defense of man, as well as the best defense and purification of the world, is accomplished by resisting the hegemony of the dogma of change, indeed, the dogma of producibility in

[10] Guardini, 10.
[11] H. Dietzfelbinger, "Dimensionen der Wahrheit", in: *Kath. Akademie in Bayern, Chronik, 1980/81*, 148–56; citation on 150.

general, and by holding fast to the rights of truth for its own sake. For in becoming true, man contributes to the world's becoming true. Moreover, if man becomes true, he also becomes good, and the world likewise becomes good around him. Thomas Aquinas, as is well known, defined truth as the adequation of the intellect to reality. The personalistic philosophy of the inter- and post-war periods has been foremost in stressing quite sharply the inadequacy of this definition.[12] Though it is certainly the case that this formula does not say everything that can be said, it does bring to light something of decisive importance: the perception of the truth is a process which brings man into conformity with being. It is a becoming one of the "I" and the world, it is consonance, it is being gifted and purified. To the extent that men allow themselves to be guided and cleansed by the truth, they find the way not only to their true selves but also to the human "thou". Truth, in fact, is the medium in which men make contact, whereas it is the absence of truth which closes them off from one another. Accordingly, movement toward the truth implies temperance. If the truth purifies man from egotism and from the illusion of absolute autonomy, if it makes him obedient and gives him the courage to be humble, it thereby also teaches him to see through producibility as a parody of freedom and to unmask undisciplined chatter as a parody of dialogue. It is victorious over the tendency to mistake the absence of all ties for freedom. Thus, the truth is fruitful precisely by being loved for its own sake.

These considerations prepare us for a final step. We must still ask Pilate's question: What is truth? Nevertheless, we must ask it differently than Pilate did. Hermann Dietzfelbinger has pointed out that the depressing thing about Pilate's question is that it is not really a question at all but an answer. Pilate's response to the One who claims to have the truth is: "Enough

---

[12] See L. B. Punzel, "Wahrheit", in: H. Krings, H. M. Baumgartner and C. Wild, *Handbuch philosophischer Grundbegriffe* 3 (Munich, 1974): 1649–68.

talk—what is truth anyway? Let's deal with the concrete instead." For the most part, Pilate's question is posed in the same form today. We, however, must now formulate it in all seriousness: How is it that to become true is to become good and that truth is good, indeed *the* good? How is it that the truth has value of itself, without having to validate itself with reference to exterior aims? These affirmations are correct only if the truth possesses its worth in itself, if it subsists in itself and has more being than everything else; if the truth itself is the ground upon which I stand. To think through the essence of truth is to arrive at the notion of God. In the long run, it is impossible to maintain the unique identity of the truth, in other words, its dignity (which in turn is the basis of the dignity both of man and of the world), without learning to perceive in it the unique identity and dignity of the living God. Ultimately, therefore, reverence for the truth is inseparable from that disposition of veneration which we call adoration. Truth and worship stand in an indissociable relationship to each other; one cannot really flourish without the other, however often they have gone their separate ways in the course of history.

4. Cult

With these last remarks we have already gained a final vantage point from which to investigate the academy and its theoretical justification. At first sight, the fact that the word "academy" was originally the name of a suburban temple precinct, which thus predates Plato's erection of his school there, may seem rather accidental to the history of the new institution. Closer examination reveals a deeper connection, which was not lost on the founder. For Plato's Academy was, from the legal point of view, a cultic association. Accordingly, the cultic veneration of the Muses was a stable component of its rhythm of life; there was a special office for preparing sacrifices.[13] This is

[13] Pieper, 37f.; cf. H. Meinhardt, "Akademie", in: J. Ritter, ed., *Historisches*

much more than an adventitious circumstance, a concession, say, to the sociological structures of the times. The freedom for the truth and the freedom of the truth cannot exist without the acknowledgment and worship of the divine. Freedom from the obligation to yield a profit can be justified and can survive only if there is something truly withdrawn from man's utility and property, hence, if the higher property right and the inviolable prerogative of the divinity perdure. "The freedom of *theoria*", says Pieper in the spirit of Plato, "is defenseless and exposed —unless it appeals in a special way to the protection of the gods."[14] Freedom from profit and emancipation from the aims of power find their deepest guarantee only in the absolute rights of the One who is not subordinate to any human power: in the freedom vis-à-vis the world which God both has and gives. For Plato, who was the first to express it philosophically, the freedom of the truth belongs not merely accidentally but essentially in the context of worship, of cult. Where the latter no longer exists, the former ceases as well. It goes without saying that worship is also nonexistent where cultic forms are indeed perpetuated but are reinterpreted as symbolic actions possessing a merely social significance. All of this means, however, that anarchic pseudofreedom is at work behind every denial of the foundations of adoration, behind every refusal of the bond to the truth and of the demands which it makes. These counterfeit freedoms, which predominate today, are the real menace to true freedom. To clarify the concept of freedom numbers among the crucial tasks of the present day—if we care about the preservation of man and of the world.

Wörterbuch der Philosophie 1 (Basel/Stuttgart, 1971): 121–24.

[14] Ibid., 36.

PART 2

THE NATURE AND
FORM OF THEOLOGY

The Spiritual Basis and Ecclesial Identity of Theology

"It is unlikely that any sensible Christian would contest that the care for the Word of God among men is entrusted to the church alone."[1] This is not the statement of some curial functionary who, hopelessly stuck in his official routine, is blind to everything but his own official competence and is no longer capable of perceiving the full scope of the issues. On the contrary, it was formulated in 1935, at the high point of the nazi campaign against the church, by a student of Rudolf Bultmann who stood at the forefront of the Confessing Evangelical Church and in an adjuratory speech was reminding the church of its responsibility for the teaching of theology. The man was Heinrich Schlier, and with these words he was giving voice to anything but purely academic theories or bureaucratic instructions. The state's attempt to convert Lutheran Christianity into a German Christianity in order to render it useful for the totalitarian rule of the party had opened his eyes, as well as those of many of his contemporaries, to the fact that theology either exists in the church and from the church, or it does not exist at all. This position is fraught with a personal destiny: the resignation of his university professorship, which his church, having grown timid and irresolute, no longer dared to support. But the theology which he thus abandoned, having withdrawn into its apparent academic freedom, had become the plaything of the ruling powers and was ready to fall prey to the might of the party.[2] This situation made it evident that the liberty

---

[1] H. Schlier, "Die Verantwortung der Kirche für den theologischen Unterricht", in: idem, *Der Geist und die Kirche*, ed. V. Kubina and K. Lehmann (Freiburg, 1980), 241–50; citation on 241. First publication Wuppertal/Barmen, 1935.

[2] Compare the chronological presentation of Schlier's life, ibid., 304. In 1935 Schlier returned his *venia legendi* ["license" to teach at the university

of theology consists in its bond to the church and that any other freedom is a betrayal both of itself and of the object entrusted to it. These circumstances revealed plainly that there can be no office of teaching theology if there is no ecclesiastical magisterium, for in its absence theology would enjoy no greater certainty than any of the liberal arts, that is, the certainty of hypothesis, which may be the subject of debate but which no one can stake his life on. Were this the case, theology would be guilty of arrogant presumption if it pretended to be anything other than the history, and possibly the psychology, sociology or at most philosophy, of Christianity.

This insight imposed itself then with burning intensity, although it was by no means acknowledged as obvious by the majority of theologians. It became the boundary line between liberal accommodation, which, in fact, quickly turned from liberality into a willingness to serve totalitarianism, and the decision for the Confessing Church, which was simultaneously a decision for a theology bound to the Creed, and, therefore, to the teaching church. Today, in outwardly peaceful times, it is not possible immediately to make out the contours in such stark relief. It is true that, on the whole, Catholic theologians would not challenge at the level of principles the Magisterium's right to exist.[3] On this point, the Church's traditional order

---

level], after his request for a leave of absence at the ecclesiastical academy had been turned down. Previously, an appointment to the University of Halle had also been denied, as had Schlier's nomination as extraordinary professor in Marburg; both on account of his belonging to the Confessing Church. A useful introduction to Schlier's thought is A. Schneider, *Wort Gottes und Kirche im theologischen Denken von H. Schlier* (Frankfurt, 1981); P. Kuhn provides a scholarly evaluation in: *Theologische Revue* 82 (1986): 31–34; also worthy of note is J. Junttila, *Corpus Christi Pneumaticum: Heinrich Schlier in käsitys kirkosta.* (Helsinki, 1981); Finnish with an ample summary in German.

[3] The present *status quæstionis* in German language theology may be gauged by consulting the work edited by W. Kern: *Die Theologie und das Lehramt* (Freiburg, 1982). Of particular importance is the substantial and judicious article by M. Seckler, "Kirchliches Lehramt und theologische Wissenschaft.

represents a prior given which for Catholics—otherwise than for the Reformed tradition—is beyond question. Nevertheless, the intrinsically necessary and positive value of the Magisterium has also lost its self-evident character in the general consciousness of today's Catholic theology. Ecclesiastical authority appears to be a tribunal wholly foreign to the nature of scientific scholarship, whose inner logic in and of itself would preclude the existence of such an authority. Scientific scholarship—so it seems—can obey only its own laws, which dictate, however, that it recognize as valid nothing except reasonable, objective argument. That some authority, taking the place of argument and of the comprehension which can be attained by argumentation, should decide what may be taught and what may not is judged to be an act contrary to scholarship: it discredits theology in the body of the university. It is said that, not authority, but arguments decide, and if, in spite of this principle, authority should attempt to make such decisions, it would be guilty of a sheer usurpation of power calling for resistance.[4]

Insofar as even Catholic theology in a great measure shares this attitude, it has entered into a contradictory situation. What Romano Guardini noted in his theology professors during the Modernist crisis and in the period immediately following it, namely, that their Catholicism was merely "liberalism kept in check by obedience to dogma", is once again—indeed, even more so—true of Catholic theology.[5] The ideas of these professors limped in either direction. Their thought could not pass

---

Geschichtliche Aspekte. Probleme und Lösungselemente" (17–62); see also M. Seckler, *Die schiefen Wände des Lehrhauses: Katholizität als Herausforderung* (Freiburg, 1988), 105–55; idem, "Theologie als Glaubenswissenschaft", in: W. Kern, H. Pottmeyer and M. Seckler, *Handbuch der Fundamentaltheologie* 4 (Freiburg, 1988): 180–241.

[4] See P. Eicher's critique of the Magisterium, which the author admittedly gives a different turn, "Von den Schwierigkeiten bürgerlicher Theologie mit den katholischen Kirchenstrukturen", in: W. Kern, 116–51.

[5] R. Guardini, *Berichte über mein Leben: Autobiographische Aufzeichnungen* (Düsseldorf, 1984), a propos of the Bonn moral theologian F. Tillmann: ". . . but

as liberalism, because it was limited by their reluctant obedience to dogma. On the other hand, it was just as incapable of recommending Catholicism as long as it was a mere fetter, and not an original principle which was positive, living and great in its own right. It is impossible to remain indefinitely in such a state of inner cleavage. If the Church and her authority constitute a factor alien to scientific scholarship, then both theology and the Church are in equal danger. In fact, a church without theology impoverishes and blinds, while a churchless theology melts away into caprice. For this reason, the question of the intrinsic connection between church and theology must be thought through from the ground up and given an unambiguous resolution; not in order to demarcate spheres of interest, or to maintain power or eliminate it, but for the sake of the rectitude of theology and ultimately of our faith itself.

The subject at hand is immense; there can be no question here of a treatment even approaching completeness. I wish merely to attempt to single out a few aspects as starting points for further reflection. In doing so, I do not intend to leave the question of the Magisterium out of consideration, but I prefer to deal with it on the margins of the present discussion. This question, in fact, is not adequately framed until we have first explained the real basis of everything else: the inner connection which binds together church and theology in their very essence. There are many ways to exhibit this connection. The collapse of the classical-liberal model between the wars, but especially during the Third Reich's antichurch campaign, afforded the most significant theologians of the time the occasion to grasp this connection and to set it forth anew, each in his own fashion. Perhaps the pioneer in this movement was the then-*privatdocent* Romano Guardini, who had transformed two events in his intellectual development into personal expe-

---

at bottom, the critical attitude was, as the later 'Bonn movement' revealed, a liberalism kept in check by obedience to dogma" (33).

rience. Kantianism had shattered the faith of his childhood, but his conversion allowed him to surmount Kant. This, in turn, was a fresh start for his thinking, which now obeyed a word spoken with authority by a living other, namely, the Church.[6] After the First World War, it was the great Evangelical exegete and historian Erik Peterson who, having discovered in controversy with Harnack and Barth the insufficiency both of the dialectical approach and its only apparent seriousness as well as of liberalism, found his way first to dogma and finally to the Catholic Church.[7] Yet even Karl Barth, likewise in dispute with Harnack, recognized after his own fashion that theology is either churchly or it simply is not theology; the fact that he entitled his magnum opus *Church Dogmatics* was and remains a profession of faith, and, without the option that this confession implies, the work would not exist.[8] Finally, we must mention the name of Heinrich Schlier: his struggle with National Socialism and his decisive refusal of a crippled academic theology led him to the new realization that theology needs the church and her authority to decide doctrine precisely because theology's sole raison d'être is "to acquire knowledge of the Word of God with order and clarity".[9] This decision, like the others, was also fraught with destiny, as we have already seen. Schlier first had to reckon with the resignation of his professorship under political persecution. Later, the road which he had thus taken

---

[6] Guardini, 32ff.; 68–72; 83–87. See also my essay: "Von der Liturgie zur Christologie: Romano Guardinis theologischer Grundansatz und seine Aussagekraft", in: J. Ratzinger, ed., *Wege zur Wahrheit. Die bleibende Bedeutung von Romano Guardini* (Düsseldorf, 1985), 128–33; H. B. Gerl, *Romano Guardini* (Mainz, 1985), 52–76.

[7] The crucial landmarks along this way are collected in: E. Peterson, *Theologische Traktate* (Munich, 1951). On Peterson's life and work, it is now possible to consult the ambitious volume of B. Pflichtweiß, *Erik Peterson: Neue Sicht auf Leben und Werk* (Freiburg, 1992).

[8] See H. U. von Balthasar, *Karl Barth: Darstellung und Deutung seiner Theologie*, 4th ed. (Einsiedeln, 1976) [H. U. von Balthasar, *The Theology of Karl Barth: Exposition and Interpretation* (San Francisco, 1992)].

[9] Schlier, 227.

brought him into the Catholic Church. It would be stimulating to elucidate and reflect upon the subject of the ecclesial identity of theology by taking the thought of these four great figures, with their antitheses and their points of convergence, as our guide.[10]

1. The New Subject as the Precondition and Foundation of All Theology

Such a method, however, would lead us much too far afield for the present. I wish, therefore, to base my treatment of the theme on something which at first glance seems to have no connection with it. In my opinion, however, this consideration actually brings us down to the foundation, which we must reflect upon in order to understand anything at all about this subject. I am referring to the statement in the Letter to the Galatians in which Saint Paul describes the distinctive element of Christianity as a personal experience which revolutionizes everything and at the same time as an objective reality: "It is no longer I who live, but Christ who lives in me" (Gal 2:20). This affirmation stands at the end of that brief spiritual autobiography which Paul sketches for his readers—not in order to boast but, by alluding to the story of his own relationship with Christ and the Church, to make clear the nature of the gospel which has been entrusted to him. Beginning on the outside, this *apologia pro vita sua* leads him, so to speak, farther and farther inward. He first presents the external events surrounding his vocation and the subsequent direction of his life. Finally, however, this one phrase, like a sudden bolt of lightning, reveals in its light the inner event which took place

---

[10] Among French-speaking theologians, Louis Bouyer should be added to this list as a figure of equal importance. Cf. the fascinating retrospect on his life's work and the comprehensive presentation of his vision of theology in the book based on conversations with G. Daix: L. Bouyer, *Le Métier du théologien* (Paris, 1979).

in those outer events and which lies at their very foundation. This inner event is at one and the same time wholly personal and wholly objective. It is an individual experience in the highest degree, yet it declares what the essence of Christianity is for everyone. To explain it as meaning that becoming and being a Christian rest upon conversion would still be much too weak a way of putting things. This is not to deny that such an interpretation is indeed aiming in the right direction, but the point is that conversion in the Pauline sense is something much more radical than, say, the revision of a few opinions and attitudes. It is a death-event. In other words, it is an exchange of the old subject for another. The "I" ceases to be an autonomous subject standing in itself. It is snatched away from itself and fitted into a new subject. The "I" is not simply submerged, but it must really release its grip on itself in order then to receive itself anew in and together with a greater "I".

In the Letter to the Galatians, the fundamental intuition about the nature of conversion—that it is the surrender of the old isolated subjectivity of the "I" in order to find oneself within the unity of a new subject, which bursts the limits of the "I", thus making possible contact with the ground of all reality—appears again with new emphases in another context. Paul, with the help of the antithesis between the law and the promise, is pursuing the question whether man can, as it were, create himself on his own or whether he must receive himself as a gift. While doing so, he emphasizes quite vigorously that the promise was issued only in the singular. It is intended, not for a mass of juxtaposed subjects, but for "the offspring of Abraham" in the singular (Gal 3:16). There is only *one* bearer of the promise, outside of which is the chaotic world of self-realization where men compete with one another and desire to compete with God but succeed merely in working right past their true hope. But in what sense is the promise the object of hope if it applies only to one individual? The Apostle's answer runs like this: "For as many of you as have been baptized into Christ have put on Christ. There is no longer Jew or Greek, there is no longer slave or free, there is no longer male or female, for you are all one [man] in Christ Jesus. And if you are Christ's, then you are Abraham's offspring, heirs according to the promise" (Gal 3:27–29). It is important to take notice of the fact that Paul does not say, for example, "you are one thing", but rather stresses that "you are one man." You have become a new, singular subject together with Christ and, in consequence—through the amalgamation of subjects—find yourselves within the purview of the promise.[11]

This second text is important because it renders explicit the objective content which is also at the basis of the first formula, "It is no longer I who live", but is not so clearly perspicuous for the reader. No one can undertake on his own the exchange of subjects spoken of by Saint Paul. Such an attempt would be illogical and absurd. Indeed, the exchange would still be the "work" of the individual subject, thus confirming his hopeless self-imprisonment. The exchange of subjects includes a passive element, which Paul rightly characterizes as death, in the sense of receiving a share in the event of the Cross. It can come to someone only from the outside, from another person. Because Christian conversion throws open the frontier between the "I" and the "not-I", it can be bestowed upon one only by the "not-I" and can never be achieved solely in the interiority of one's personal decision. It has a sacramental structure. The "I no longer live" does not describe a private mystical experience but rather defines the essence of baptism.[12] What takes place is a sacramental event, hence, an event involving the Church. The passive side of becoming a Christian calls for the acting Church, in which the unity of believers as a single subject manifests itself in its bodily and historical dimensions.

---

[11] On the exegesis of Galatians 2:20: H. Schlier, *Der Brief an die Galater* (Göttingen, 1962), 101–4; F. Mußner, *Der Galaterbrief* (Freiburg, 1974), 182–87. Both commentaries may also be consulted in reference to the other texts of the Letter to the Galatians discussed here.

[12] H. Schlier, *Der Brief an die Galater*, 102.

Only in this way is it possible to understand adequately the Pauline designation of the Church as the "body of Christ". This expression is synonymous with putting on Christ, or better, with being clothed with Christ. The new clothing meant here, which both veils Christians and at the same time gives them freedom of movement, is the new bodiliness of Christ, new because it is his risen body.

Whoever reads Paul in this perspective comes upon the same basic intuition again and again, expressed from the most diverse points of view. In the baptismal theology of the Letter to the Romans, it is linked to the idea of tradition, that is, to the contents of the Christian's knowledge and profession. This Letter describes baptism as an experience of being committed to the standard of doctrine; the subjective response to this transaction, in which one is handed over into a common sphere of knowledge, is an obedience coming from the heart (Rom 6:17).[13] The same idea is presented from yet another angle in the First Letter to the Corinthians, wherein Paul unfolds the likeness of the body and its members, which was current in ancient social philosophy. Its application to the Church results in a surprising twist which is overlooked by most commentators. This omission necessarily leads, in turn, to a misinterpretation of the fundamental principles of Pauline ecclesiology, which, though it is by no means ashamed to borrow from the social theory of the times, derives from an entirely different basic conception. For Paul does not say "as in an organism there are many members working in harmony, so too in the Church", as if he were proposing a purely sociological model of the Church, but at the very moment when he leaves behind the ancient simile, he shifts the idea to an entirely different level. He affirms, in fact, that, just as there is one body but many members, "so it is with Christ" (1 Cor 12:12). The

---

[13] H. Schlier, *Der Römerbrief* (Freiburg, 1977), 207–10; E. Käsemann, *An die Römer* (Tübingen, 1973), 171f. [E. Käsemann, *Commentary on Romans* (London, 1980)].

term of the comparison is not the Church, since, according to Paul, the Church is in no wise a separate subject endowed with its own subsistence. The new subject is much rather "Christ" himself, and the Church is nothing but the space of this new unitary subject, which is, therefore, much more than mere social interaction. It is an application of the same christological singular found in the Letter to the Galatians. Here, too, it has a sacramental reference, though this time it points to the Eucharist, whose essence Paul defines two chapters before in the bold assertion: "Because there is one bread, we who are many are one body" (10:17). "One body": in accordance with the biblical significance of *soma*, this may be translated as "one subject", provided we are sensitive to the connotations of bodiliness and historicity belonging to this word.

Before we ask ourselves what all of this actually has to do with theology, I would like, at least in passing, to allude to the way in which the same reality is reflected in the Gospel of John. If, in fact, Paul is concerned above all with the problem of faith and of the profession which pertains to it, John poses quite incisively the problem of right understanding, though both are ultimately concerned with the truth of our being. John is confronted with the fact that all purely empirical—we would say, "purely historical"—talk about Jesus is caught in an absurd tangle of misunderstandings. Such an approach to the question of Jesus' identity reduces it to the question of his real origins. We are already face to face with the typical historicist misapprehension which believes that it has explained a fact by analyzing the process of its origin and development. For John, this is a gross error. If, however, it is not possible to come to know Jesus in the true sense by throwing light on his origins, that is, by retracing his history, what are the right means? John gives an answer which at first must strike modern thinking as mythological. He affirms that only the Paraclete, the Spirit, who is the Spirit both of the Father and of the Son himself, can make Jesus known. Someone can be understood only through himself. Closer attention soon reveals that the reference to the Spirit is an initiation into ecclesiology and that John thus has in mind a precisely defined process of understanding. For how does the Spirit operate? First of all, by bestowing remembrance, a remembrance in which the particular is joined to the whole, which in turn endows the particular, which hitherto had not been understood, with its genuine meaning. A further characteristic of the Spirit is listening: he does not speak in his own name, he listens and teaches how to listen. In other words, he does not add anything but rather acts as a guide into the heart of the Word, which becomes light in the act of listening. The Spirit does not employ violence; his method is simply to allow what stands before me as an other to express itself and to enter into me. This already entails an additional element: the Spirit effects a space of listening and remembering, a "we", which in the Johannine writings defines the Church as the locus of knowledge. Understanding can take place only within this "we" constituted by participation in the origin. Indeed, all comprehension depends on participation. Bultmann elucidates this point admirably when he says, regarding John's conception of the witness of the Spirit: "[I]t is 'repetition', a 'calling to mind' in the light of their present relationship with him." [14]

2. Conversion, Faith and Thought

Although this whole reflection is, on the face of it, rather far removed from our usual questions about the concept and methods of theology, nevertheless the relevant connections are gradually beginning to delineate themselves. Let us start with a seeming commonplace: theology presupposes faith. It draws its life from

---

[14] R. Bultmann, *Das Evangelium nach Johannes*, 15th ed. (Göttingen, 1957), 427 [*The Gospel of John. A Commentary* (Oxford, 1971), 554]; regarding what I have developed here about John, cf. the fine article of H. Schlier, "Der Heilige Geist als Interpret nach dem Johannesevangelium", in: *Der Geist und die Kirche*, 165–78.

the paradoxical union of faith and science. Whoever pretends to abolish this paradox does away with theology and also ought to have the courage to admit it. Whoever, on the other hand, embraces it in principle is bound to accept its inherent tensions. This paradox brings to light the special nature of Christianity's claim to truth and the specific character of the Christian faith with respect to the whole history of religion. For theology, in the strict sense of the word, is an exclusively Christian phenomenon, which has no exact equivalent in other religions. These affirmations presuppose that faith regards the truth, by which I mean a kind of knowledge which does not concern the functioning of this or that particular thing, but the truth of our being itself. Thus, faith concerns what we must do to attain the rectitude of our being. These assertions also presuppose that this truth becomes accessible only in the act of faith and that faith is the gift of a new beginning for thought which it is not in our power either to set in existence or to replace. At the very same time, however, they take it for granted that, once accepted, this truth illuminates our whole being and, therefore, also appeals to our intellect and even solicits our understanding. It is assumed that this truth addresses itself as such to reason and requires the activity of reason in order to become man's own possession and to deploy its full dynamism. Whereas myth, whether in Greece or India, does no more than multiply images of the truth, which for its part always remains incomprehensible, faith in Christ, as it is expressed in its basic assertions, is never interchangeable. True, faith does not remove the essential limitation of man in his relation to the truth: it does not, in other words, eliminate the law of analogy. Nevertheless, analogy is not the same as metaphor. Analogy can always be broadened and deepened, but, within the boundaries of man's possibilities, it declares the very truth. In this sense, rationality belongs to the essence of Christianity in a way which the other religions do not claim for themselves. Any attempt to restrain its movement would amount to opposition to an indispensable dimension of the faith. Therein lies the limit which the Magisterium of the Church must bear in mind in its partnership with theology.

First, however, we must fill out the idea which emerged in outline from the sketch of Paul and John. We are now in a position to say that both faith and rational reflection are integral to theology. The absence of either principle would bring about theology's demise. This implies that theology is based upon a new beginning in thought which is not the product of our own reflection but has its origin in the encounter with a Word which always precedes us.[15] We call the act of accepting this new beginning "conversion". Because there is no theology without faith, there can be no theology without conversion. Conversion can take many forms. It need not always be an instantaneous event, as it was in the case of Augustine or Pascal, Newman or Guardini. In one form or another, however, the convert must consciously pronounce in his own name a Yes to this new beginning and really turn from the "I" to the "no-longer-I". It is thus immediately obvious that the opportunity for creative theology increases the more that faith becomes real, personal experience; the more that conversion acquires interior certainty thanks to a painful process of transformation; the more that it is recognized as the indispensable means of penetrating into the truth of one's own being. This is why in every age the path to faith can take its bearings by converts; it explains why they in particular can help us to recognize the reason for the hope that is in us (cf. 1 Pet 3:15) and to bear witness to it. The connection between faith and theology is not, therefore, some sort of sentimental or pietistic twaddle but is a direct consequence of the logic of the thing and is corroborated by the whole of history. Athanasius is inconceivable without Anthony, the father of monasticism, and the latter's new experience of Christ;[16] Augustine is likewise

---

[15] R. Guardini has stressed this quite energetically in his little book: *Das Bild von Jesus dem Christus im Neuen Testament* (Herderbücherei, 1962), 138−41.

[16] On this relationship, see the very illuminating article of J. Roldanus, "Die

unthinkable without his passionate journey to a radical Christian life. Moreover, Bonaventure and the Franciscan theology of the thirteenth century would have been impossible without the imposing new representation of Christ in the figure of Saint Francis of Assisi, nor could Thomas Aquinas have existed without Dominic's breakthrough to the gospel and to evangelization. One could continue in this vein along the whole course of history. Pure rationality is not itself sufficient to bring forth great Christian theology: at bottom, even such outstanding figures as Ritschl, Jülicher, and Harnack appear curiously empty theologically when we read them from the distance of later generations. Naturally, the opposite is also true: a nervously introverted piety is incapable of a testimony which restores to faith fresh power to convince and thereby to become once again a message reaching out beyond its own frontiers to mankind in search of the truth.

3. The Ecclesial Character of Conversion and Its Consequences for Theology

These considerations already carry us a step farther. We said that faith requires conversion and that conversion is an act of obedience toward a reality which precedes me and which does not originate from me. Moreover, this obedience continues, inasmuch as knowledge never transforms this reality into a constituent element of my own thought, but rather the converse is true: it is I who make myself over to it, while it always remains above me. For Christians, this prior reality is not an "it" but a "he" or, even better, a "thou". It is Christ, the Word made flesh. He is the new beginning of our thought. He is the new "I" which bursts open the limits of subjectivity

---

Vita Antonii als Spiegel der Theologie des Athanasius", in: *Theol. Phil* (1983), 194–216.

and the boundaries dividing subject from object, thus enabling me to say: "It is no longer I who live."

From this vantage point, perspectives open up in various directions. I shall attempt to do no more than allude to them very briefly. In the first place, the "we character" of this event is evident. Conversion does not lead into a private relationship with Jesus, which in reality would be another form of mere monologue. It is delivery into the pattern of doctrine, as Paul says, or, as we discovered in John, entrance into the "we" of the Church. This is the sole guarantee that the obedience which we owe to the truth is concrete. Guardini in particular set forth repeatedly this nucleus of his conversion experience, which became the center of his own theology and, after the shipwreck of the liberal model, offered a fresh start to theology as a whole. The word at the heart of his conversion, which proved to be the turning point of his life, was Matthew 10:39: "He who finds his life [whoever would realize himself] will lose it, and he who loses his life for my sake will find it." In the wake of his vain attempts at self-realization, this word had burned itself into his soul with an unquestionable human evidence. It is necessary to lose oneself in order to find oneself. But where? The answer certainly cannot be indifferent. This sort of loss can have only *one* suitable addressee: God. But where is God? Here is Guardini's experience in his own words: "There is no 'easy access' God. In contrast to the pretension of the autonomous search for God, . . . he is the unknown God, who 'dwells in unapproachable light' (1 Tim 6:16)."[17] Only the concrete God can be something other than a new projection of one's own self. Following in Christ's footsteps is the only way of losing oneself which attains the desired goal. But at this point yet another question arises: Which image of

---

[17] Guardini's conversion experience is sketched in: *Berichte über mein leben*, 71ff. H. B. Gerl has shown that Guardini returned again and again to Matthew 10:39 (44f.); in his last book: *Die Kirche des Herrn* (Würzburg, 1965), Guardini once again offers an impressive exegesis of the text; see p. 62 of the same for the passage cited here.

Jesus is more than an image? Where can I find the real Jesus and not merely ideas about him? Guardini, commenting upon the plurality of Christ images, observes: "A more searching examination, however, discovers once again that disquieting similarity of the various images of Christ to whoever happens to have sketched them. One often has the impression that these figures of Christ are the idealized self-portraits of their authors."[18] And the answer? The one who became flesh has remained flesh. He is concrete. "Christ's Church never ceases to challenge the individual to give his own life, so that he might receive it again in a new and authentic form."[19] Obedience to the Church is the concreteness of our obedience. The Church is that new and greater subject in which past and present, subject and object come into contact. The Church is our contemporaneity with Christ: there is no other.[20]

The key word "incarnation" discloses further insights, which Heinrich Schlier has developed in detail in his account of his conversion.[21] There is time only to mention them in passing here. First of all, there is the correlation of tradition and living transmission. Intrinsically connected to this is apostolic authority, which interprets the Word which is handed down and gives it an unequivocal clarity of meaning. Finally, there is the insight that God has definitively decided in our favor. "According to the New Testament", this decidedness accounts for "the fact that the faith fixes itself in concrete propositions which demand from belief concrete acknowledgment of their truth."[22] It is for this reason that Schlier could say that he had become a Catholic by strictly Protestant means —namely, *sola scriptura*. Whoever had the privilege of being his friend knew that he had lost nothing of the greatness of his

[18] *Die Kirche des Herrn*, 63.

[19] Ibid., 64.

[20] Cf. ibid., 67–70.

[21] H. Schlier, *Kurze Rechenschaft*, republished in: *Der Geist und die Kirche*, 270–89.

[22] Ibid., 279.

Protestant heritage but had merely brought it to its ultimate conclusion.

This is a good place to interrupt the course of my reflections, since the decisive point has already been clarified: the Church is not an authority which remains foreign to the scientific character of theology but is rather the ground of theology's existence and the condition which makes it possible. The Church, moreover, is not an abstract principle but a living subject possessing a concrete content. This subject is by nature greater than any individual person, indeed, than any single generation. Faith is always participation in a totality and, precisely in this way, conducts the believer to a new breadth of freedom. On the other hand, the Church is not an intangible spiritual realm in which everyone can pick what suits him. She is endowed with a concreteness rooted in the binding Word of faith. And she is a living voice which pronounces itself in the organs of the faith.[23]

4. Faith, Proclamation and Theology

It is not necessary at this time to expound in detail the theory of the Magisterium and its forms which follows from what we have just said. Nevertheless, we must still deal with a few concrete issues which crop up continually in this context. For the problems lie in the concrete. It is not at all difficult to acknowledge in theory that theology is ecclesial by its very nature; that the Church does not merely provide theology with an organizational framework but is its inner foundation and its immediate wellspring; that, in consequence, the Church cannot be incompetent in matters of content or theologically mute but must have a living voice, that is, the faculty to speak bindingly even for the theologian. However, another means of es-

[23] R. Guardini developed the idea of the Church as the subject of theology in his Bonn inaugural lecture: "Anselm von Canterbury und das Wesen der Theologie", in: *Auf dem Wege: Versuche* (Mainz, 1923).

caping this concreteness, an expedient which increasingly finds public advocates today, insinuates itself here. The pastoral office, it is said, is entrusted to the Church; she preaches for the faithful but does not teach for the theologians. But such a divorce of preaching and teaching is most profoundly opposed to the essence of the biblical message. It merely rehashes that division between psychics and gnostics whereby the so-called gnosis of antiquity had already tried to secure for itself a free zone, which in reality placed it outside of the Church and her faith. This division, in fact, presupposes the typically pagan way of conceiving the relationship between myth and philosophy, religious symbolism and enlightened reason. Christianity's critique of religion ran counter to this scheme and was accordingly also a critique of a certain religious class mentality. It achieved the emancipation of the simple and credited even them with the capacity to be philosophers in the true sense of the word, that is, to lay hold of the essential dimension of man's being, and to do so as well as or even better than the learned. Jesus' words concerning the incomprehension of the wise and the understanding of the "babes" (especially Mt 11:25, par.) are pertinent precisely to this situation, inasmuch as they establish Christianity as a popular religion, as a religious creed without any two-caste system.

As a matter of fact, proclamation in the form of preaching does teach bindingly; such is its essence. For it does not suggest some sort of pastime or a kind of religious entertainment. Its aim is to tell man who he is and what he must do to be himself. Its intention is to disclose to him the truth about himself, that is, what he can base his life on and what he can die for. No one dies for interchangeable myths; if one myth leads to difficulties, there is always another to select in its place. Nor is it possible to live on hypotheses: after all, life itself is no hypothesis but rather unrepeatable reality upon which rides an eternal destiny.[24] But how could the Church teach bindingly if at the same time her

---

[24] R. Spaemann offers a brilliant analysis of the civilization of hypothesis,

teaching remained without binding force for theologians? The essence of the Magisterium consists precisely in the fact that the proclamation of the faith is also the normative criterion of theology: indeed, this very proclamation is the object of theological reflection. In this sense, the faith of the simple is not a sort of theology whittled down to the measure of the layman, a kind of "Platonism for the people". On the contrary, things stand in precisely the reverse relationship: proclamation is the measure of theology, and not vice versa. This primacy of simple faith, moreover, is also in perfect accord with a fundamental anthropological law: the great truths about human nature are grasped in a simple apprehension which is in principle available to everyone and which is never wholly retrieved in reflection. One could say—somewhat carelessly—that the Creator has, as it were, proceeded in a thoroughly democratic fashion. Though not all men can be professional theologians, access to the great fundamental cognitions is open to everyone. In this sense, the Magisterium has something like a democratic character: it defends the common faith, which recognizes no distinction of rank between the learned and the simple. It is indeed true that in virtue of her pastoral office the Church is empowered to preach and not to teach scientific theology. The point, however, is that the very office of preaching the gospel is the teaching office even for theology.

This observation already touches upon an aspect of the question which was raised earlier. We had said that it is not difficult to accept the Magisterium in theory. But the passage from theory to practice immediately arouses a grave misgiving: Is it not the case that this transition unduly restricts thought's freedom of movement? Does it not inevitably give rise to a minute supervision which takes up the breathing space needed for great thought? Must we not fear that the Church may also interfere beyond the confines of preaching in the proper busi-

"Die christliche Religion und das Ende des modernen Bewußtseins", in: *IKZ Communio* 8 (1979): 251–70, esp. 264–68.

ness of the scholar and thus overreach herself? These questions must be taken seriously. In consequence, it is legitimate
to seek to regulate the relationship between theology and the
Magisterium in such a way as to guarantee that the inherent
responsibility of theology have its due sphere of action. Yet,
however warranted this procedure may be, the limitations of
such ways of framing the issues must be borne in mind. In
reality, whoever sees ecclesial identity as nothing but a fetter is
already operating on a false conception of theology. This was
the insight which had dawned upon Guardini in the encounter
with his professors, who, though personally orthodox, in their
scholarly work were emulators of liberalism. This insight led
him to a radically new beginning: If theology considers its own
specific property only as an obstacle, how can it possibly yield
any fruit? We must factor Church and dogma into the theological equation as a generative power rather than as a shackle. Indeed, only this "energy source" discloses to theology its grand
perspectives.[25] As an example, let us take exegesis, which even
today is considered to be the classic illustration of the fact that
the Church is a mere hindrance to theology. What, then, does
a theology which emancipates itself from the Church actually
achieve? In what sort of freedom does it then find itself? It
becomes antiquarianism. It limits its researches to the past and
advances varying hypotheses regarding the origin of individual texts and their relationship to the historical facts. These
hypotheses interest us more than other literary theories only
because the Church still asserts that these books document not
merely past events but what is true. Neither does the attempt
to make the Bible relevant by means of some personal philosophy improve matters, for there are better philosophies which
nonetheless leave us cold. But how exciting exegesis becomes
when it dares to read the Bible as a unified whole. If the Bible
originates from the one subject formed by the people of God
and, through it, from the divine subject himself, then it speaks

---

[25] Cf. *Berichte über mein Leben*, 86 and passim.

of the present. If this is so, moreover, even what we know about the diversity of its underlying historical constellations yields its harvest; there is a unity to be discovered in this diversity, and diversity appears as the wealth of unity. This opens up a wide field of action both to historical research and to its hypotheses, with the sole limit that it may not destroy the unity of the whole, which is situated on another plane than what can be called the "nuts and bolts" of the various texts. Unity is found on another plane, yet it belongs to the literary reality of the Bible itself.

Let me mention briefly one more example. When New Testament criticism began to uncover before our eyes the various layers of testimony about Christ, it opened up vistas which permitted us to see Jesus in a new way and to discover in him aspects which had gone unnoticed until then. But when one commences peeling these layers from one another and begins to identify the truth with the conjectured antiquity of origin, the image of Christ is progressively impoverished until in the end nothing is left but a few hypotheses. How stimulating, how wonderful it would be to renew the quest for that Jesus who is portrayed, not by this or that presumed source, but by the real New Testament itself. An additional element makes an unexpected appearance: the dismemberment of the Bible has led to a new variety of allegorism. One no longer reads the text but the supposed experience of supposed communities. The result is an often highly fanciful allegorical interpretation, which turns out to be a means of self-affirmation for the interpreter. For a long time it seemed as if the Magisterium, that is, the Church's proclamation of faith, compelled a superimposition of dogma on the biblical text and thus obstructed an unbiased historical interpretation of Scripture. Today the evidence shows that only mooring in the Church's faith safeguards the historical weight of the text and makes possible an adherence to the letter which is not fundamentalism. For without the living subject, either one must absolutize the letter, or else it vanishes into indefiniteness.

This is a further corroboration of what we saw while considering how conversion, faith and theology intimately hang together, namely, that theology has burgeoned, never by dissociating itself from the Church, but by turning back to it. Alienation from the Church has invariably impoverished and flattened theological reflection. The great blossoming of theology between the world wars, which made possible the Second Vatican Council, once again bears powerful witness in our century to this connection. Now, this is by no means intended as a sort of apotheosis of the Magisterium. The danger of a narrowminded and petty surveillance is no figment of the imagination, as the history of the Modernist controversy demonstrates—even though the summary judgments which are so widespread today are too unilateral to do justice to the seriousness of the issue. Needless to say, a dismissal of the Magisterium along with doctrinal discipline would as little resolve this question as denying the existence of the problems.

With regard to this last point, permit me to return to Heinrich Schlier. Schlier's theological addresses from the years 1935 and 1936 are first of all representative of the believing struggle of Evangelical Christians for their Christian identity against the assault of totalitarian might. Beyond their immediate scope, however, they mark that courage of the theologian who convicts pseudotheology of its falsity and exposes the spurious courage of the heretical misappropriation of the faith. Facing a situation in which the official organs of the church in large measure still kept silence and, owing to their fear and halfheartedness, left the way wide open for the misuse of Christian values, Schlier appealed directly to the students of theology in the following words:

> Consider for a moment which is better: that, after mature reflection, the church, following an established procedure, remove a theologian's authorization to teach because of false doctrine, or that the individual take it into his own hands to denounce this or that theologian as a false teacher and warn against him.

After all, one must not believe that condemnation ceases when everyone is allowed to judge as he thinks fit. This is merely a logical application of the liberal view that there is no such thing as a decision about the truth of a doctrine, so that every doctrine is true to a certain extent and every doctrine is to be tolerated in the church. We, however, do not share this notion, for it denies that God has really decided among us.[26]

From today's vantage point, it is easy to say that at that time it truly was a question of whether the church would continue to proclaim the gospel of Christ or become a tool of the Antichrist. It is easy to say that even an apparent liberalism was actually serving the cause of the Antichrist. Yet at the historical juncture when man must act, there are always a thousand reasons for and against. There is no geometrical proof which would render decision superfluous. The evidence of faith is not the evidence of geometry: it is always possible to circumvent it with some dialectical maneuver. This is precisely why there exists the commission of the apostolic office, which after painstaking scrutiny casts the internal evidence of the faith in the form of a decision. It is doubtless important to find juridical procedures which safeguard within its limits the proper autonomy of scholarly reflection and ensure the free space needed for scientific discussion. However, the liberty of the individual who happens to be teaching is neither the only nor even the supreme right which requires protection in this area. In relation to the hierarchy of values in the New Testament, the Lord makes an uncompromising declaration whose seriousness

---

[26] These are the terms of the lecture which Schlier delivered in 1936 at the conference of theological students of the Rhineland: "Die kirchliche Verantwortung des Theologiestudenten", in: *Der Geist und die Kirche*, 225–40; the citation is found on 232. In midst of the postconciliar controversy, Schlier took up this idea of decision once again and developed it systematically in his fundamental article: "Das bleibend Katholische. Ein Versuch über ein Prinzip des Katholischen" (1970), in: idem, *Das Ende der Zeit. Exegetische Aufsätze und Vorträge* 3 (Freiburg, 1971): 297–320.

the Church cannot evade: "Whoever causes one of these little ones who believe in me to sin [scandalizes one of these little ones . . .], it would be better for him if a great millstone were hung round his neck and he were thrown into the sea" (Mk 9:42). In the context of this verse, "little ones" does not mean children but is the name which in Jesus' language designates his disciples, the future Christians. And the scandal which threatens them does not refer to sexual temptations but rather to the stumbling block which leads to the loss of faith. According to the findings of contemporary exegesis, "to give scandal" signifies "to dissuade from believing" and thereby to "deprive of eternal salvation".[27] The highest ranking good, for which the Church bears responsibility, is the faith of the simple. Reverence for this faith must also be the inner criterion of all theological teaching as well. Whoever does not pursue purely private research, but teaches in the name of the Church, must be cognizant of this. Accepting this commission and speaking, not in one's own name, but in the name of the common subject, the Church, includes an obligation whereby the individual imposes limits upon himself. This is so because, along with the commission, he is also entrusted with an authority which, as a private scholar and without the confidence men place in the Church's word, he would not enjoy. Together with authority he is invested with a power which is simultaneously a responsibility, inasmuch as it does not derive from him but rests upon his mission—upon the Church's name, in which he is now permitted to speak. Those who talk nowadays of the abuse of power connected with doctrinal discipline in the Church generally have in mind only the misuse of authority on the part of the Church's ministerial office, which doubtless can occur. But it is entirely forgotten that there is also a misemployment of the authority conferred by one's mission: the exploitation

---

[27] See R. Pesch, *Das Markusevangelium* 2 (Freiburg, 1977): 114, with reference to G. Stählin, *ThWNT* 7, column 351 (σκανδαλον κτλ.).

of the readiness to listen and to trust, which even today men still manifest toward the pronouncements of the Church, for a purely private utterance. Ecclesiastical authority actively serves this misappropriation of power when, by giving it free reign, it makes its own prestige available where it has absolutely no right to do so. The solicitude for the faith of the little ones must be more important in its eyes than the opposition of the great.

I would like to stop here, because the particular questions touching the best way to guarantee in practice the various rights at issue involve us in problems of application which exceed the framework of this discussion. On the other hand, when all concerned allow themselves to be guided by conscience and express in their mutual dealings the basic act of conversion to the Lord, which is common to all, there can be no insoluble difficulties, even though conflicts will never be totally absent. The state of theology and the Church will be so much the better the more the bond to the Lord inspires the thought and action of all parties; the more each individual can say like Paul: "It is no longer I who live. . . ."

5. The Temptation and Greatness of Theology

Permit me to conclude with a little episode in which these issues took on visible form for me. On the occasion of a talk which I gave in southern Italy, I had the opportunity to visit the magnificent Romanesque cathedral of Troia, a small town located in Apulia. What particularly captured my attention on the inside of the cathedral was a somewhat enigmatic relief on the pulpit, dating from the year 1158. Long before my visit, a friend had already awakened my interest in it, because, according to his interpretation, it was an allegorical depiction of theology which signified a true *laus theologiæ*—a celebration of theology in the Church and for the Church. This relief shows three

beasts whose reciprocal relationship was evidently intended by
the artist to portray the situation of the Church of his day. At
the very bottom, one sees a lamb upon which a huge lion has
greedily pounced. The lion is holding it fast in its powerful
claws and its teeth. The lamb's body is already torn open. Its
bones are visible and it is obvious that bits of flesh have already
been gobbled away. Only the infinitely mournful gaze of the
little beast assures the onlooker that the lamb, though almost
torn to pieces, is still alive. In contrast to the impotence of the
lamb, the lion is the expression of brute violence, to which
the lamb can oppose nothing but helpless fear. It is clear that
the lamb represents the Church, or, better, the faith which is
of and in the Church. What the sculpture conveys, then, is a
sort of "report on the state of the faith" which seems to be
extraordinarily pessimistic. It is the Church in her essence, the
Church of faith, which appears already half-devoured by the
lion, the symbol of power, in whose clutches it is held prisoner.
All it can do now is endure its fate in defenseless misery. But
the sculpture, which depicts with due realism the hopelessness
of the Church's situation from a human point of view, is also
an expression of the hope which knows that faith is invincible.
This hope is represented in a remarkable way: a third animal,
a small white dog, is falling upon the lion. Though it seems
no equal match for the strength of the lion, the dog throws
itself with tooth and claw upon the monster. Perhaps it too
will become the lion's prey, but its attack will oblige the beast
to release the lamb.

Whereas the significance of the lamb is in some sense clear,
the question remains to be answered: Who is the lion? Who
is the small white dog? So far I have not been able to consult any reference work of art history on this point; nor do I
know from which source the friend whom I mentioned before drew his explanation of the image. Therefore, I must
leave the problem of its correct historical interpretation un-
resolved. Since the work stems from the Hohenstaufen pe-

riod, one could think that in some way it displays the struggle between imperial power and the Church. It is probably more accurate, however, to interpret the whole piece in the light of the classical symbolic language of Christian iconography.[28] In this language, the lion can represent the devil, or else—more concretely—heresy, which rips out the Church's flesh, tears it to pieces and devours it hungrily. The white hound symbolizes fidelity. It is the sheep dog, which stands for the shepherd himself: "The good shepherd lays down his life for the sheep" (Jn 10:11). We must still answer one question: Where does theology find itself in the dramatic melee of these three creatures? In my friend's opinion, the small, courageous dog, which rescues faith from the deadly grip of the lion, is a likeness of sacred doctrine. For my part, the more I reflect, the more it seems to me that the sculpture—supposing it is even legitimate to interpret it along these lines—rather leaves the issue unsettled. The image is not simply a celebration of theology but a challenge, an examination of conscience, a question in suspense. Only the significance of the lamb is clearly defined. The other two animals, the lion and the dog—do they not stand for the two possible forms of theology, for the opposite courses which it can take? The lion—is it not the embodiment of the historical temptation of theology to make itself the lord of faith? Does it not personify the *violentia rationis*, which Bonaventure would describe a century later as an abortive form of theological reflection?[29] As for the brave hound—it stands for the opposite choice, for a theology which understands itself to be the servant of the faith and for that reason agrees to make itself a laughingstock by putting the intemperance and tyranny of naked reason in their place. If this exegesis is correct, what a question the relief on the Troia pulpit poses to preachers and

[28] Cf. in J. Siebert, *Lexikon christlicher Kunst* (Freiburg, 1980), the following articles: "Hund" [dog] (149) and "Löwe" [lion] (207f.).

[29] Bonaventura, *Sent.*, prooem. q 2 ad 6.

theologians of all times! It is an examination of conscience for pastors and for theologians, since both can be ravening predators or protectors of the flock. Hence this image, as a question which is never closed, concerns us all.[30]

---

[30] G. Biffi, taking as his point of departure a similar analogy, has wittily illustrated the connection between theology and the Church, *La bella, la bestia e il cavaliere: Saggio di teologia inattuale* (Milan, 1984).

Pluralism as a Problem
for Church and Theology

1. The Limit of the Church's Claim
and the Plurality of Human Options

The catchword "pluralism" was elaborated in turn-of-the-century England—in particular by H. Laski—for use in the political-social sphere.[1] It was set in opposition to a doctrine of sovereignty according to which separate individuals stood alone before the state and its pretensions to supreme power. In contrast to this absolute claim on the part of the state, pluralism means that each individual belongs to a plurality of social groupings and that this plurality gives rise to a multiplicity of social roles, none of which can absorb man entirely. In this perspective, the state is simply one grouping among others. It cannot exercise ultimate authority over man but can lay claim to him only in one precisely defined role, which exists side by side with his various other roles. The network of concurring roles is accordingly conceived as an order of freedom. Man always remains more than any role; he cannot be totally taken in at any point. The plurality of the representatives of this order who have a share in the formation of social life acts as a guarantee against the concentration of power and ideally ensures breathing space for the intimate sphere of the personality. Such conceptions, which were decidedly contrary to Enlightenment ideas regarding the state, had found support in researches on the social system of the Middle Ages and, to that extent, were entirely in continuity with Christian political and social traditions. Moreover, since the nineteenth century,

---

[1] Cf. P. Henrici, "Kirche und Pluralismus", in: *IKZ Communio* 12 (1983): 97–100 [P. Henrici, "The Church and Pluralism", in: *Communio International Catholic Review* 10 (1983): 128–32]; C. Graf von Krockow, "Pluralismus", in: *RGG* 5:421f. (Lit.).

Catholic social teaching had pursued similar lines of thought. The confinement of the state's authority to the domain rightly belonging to it and the emphasis on social entities outside its immediate scope number among the oldest constants of Christian solicitude for the right ordering of the commonwealth.[2]

Nevertheless, the inner logic of the ideas of Laski and of kindred thinkers made it inevitable that they would one day pose a question for the Church as well. If every social body is merely relative, if it is entitled to demand obedience only within its legitimate competence and the social role connected with it, must this not also apply to the Church? Must not even the Church, then, regard herself as one association among others possessing a correspondingly limited authority? Must it not follow that the conscience, the ultimate and most intimate element of personhood, counts even for the Church as something inviolable and untouchable above every social role? Must not the Church keep to the sphere of interests and needs delegated to her, that is, the regulation of the religious need? At this point, however, the opposite question arises: What is this religious need, this religious interest? Is it a circumscribed need alongside of and together with others, like the need for food, clothing, recreation, professional fulfillment, and so on? Or is not the religious need the expression of man's ultimate, characteristic bond, which affects his very being in its entirety? Consequently, is not the community ordered to this ultimate need—a need which brings into play the discovery of man's identity—also ipso facto where man truly finds out who he is and thereby proves himself superior to every role? In what other setting and by what other means could man ever transcend his roles and always maintain his own identity no matter where and when he plays them? In fine, must not the commu-

---

[2] Cf. J. Höffner, *Christliche Gesellschaftslehre* textbook ed. (Cologne, 1975); C. Ruhnau, *Der Katholizismus in der sozialen Bewährung* (Paderborn, 1980); on the historical roots, see the classic work of O. von Gierke, *Das deutsche Genossenschaftsrecht*, 4 vol. (Berlin, 1868–1913).

nity established to provide for this need be wholly different in kind from all other communities?

The questions raised by Laski's school had at first very little impact on Central Europe, where a new interest in the conception of authority predominated between the two world wars. In the 1920s, the critique of Carl Schmitt, the creator of political theology, who attributed a demoralizing influence to pluralistic ideas, was favored with widespread agreement.[3] Only after the totalitarian systems had perpetrated a monstrous perversion of authority into authoritarianism did a new situation arise in Central Europe as well: the image of society now corresponded to the pluralistic model. From the legal and social point of view, the churches became a kind of association; this was the social status which enabled them to assert their freedom of movement and to develop their autonomy toward the state. But did this not also oblige them really to comport themselves as associations, even internally? Was the Church entitled to extend her claim to obedience any farther than did, for example, a trade union? Could the Church demand any other attention than the other interest groups when she issued her moral imperatives to the legislator? Whoever, presupposing such parameters of comparison, wishes to justify, say, doctrinal liberty in the Church must be reminded that no party or lobby could tolerate the sort of pluralism of doctrinal opinions regarding its internal positions which we observe in today's Church. Should it exist, any common advocacy of interests would be illusory.

Before we pursue this idea any further, we must consider yet another development which has meanwhile taken place in society and the Church.[4] In fact, side by side with the quest for pluralism, an ever more powerful movement toward uni-

---

[3] C. Schmitt, *Staatsethik und pluralistischer Staat*, Kantstudien 35 (1930), 28–42.

[4] In what follows, I pursue ideas which I first developed in: Internationale Theologenkommission, *Die Einheit des Glaubens und der theologische Pluralismus* (Einsiedeln, 1973), 11–16.

formity is taking place in the modern world. Ever more massive economic and political amalgamations together with corresponding concentrations of power are emerging. The mass media are fostering a tendency toward homogeneity in thought, speech and behavior which would have been inconceivable in earlier periods. This standardization of man, whose formative influence reaches from the outside down to his unconscious life, is an extension of the communication which has already been achieved in the shaping of the world by technology; for its part, this communication is founded upon the mathematical decoding of nature. Whereas the great philosophies always retained a certain particularity, the mathematically based physical sciences and the technical disciplines are almost devoid of cultural peculiarity. This uniformity is possible, however, only because technological civilization limits itself to a quite definite sector of man's knowledge of reality. Technical civilization is innately positivistic, by which I mean that it embraces only that section of reality which can be subjected to the positive method, that is, to the criterion of falsifiability. Everyone knows how much this method can accomplish: we have firsthand experience of its success in our everyday life, which to a great extent is shaped by these achievements. On the other hand, we also perceive in the subterranean rumbling of the human organism, indeed, of the earth on which we live and of the air which we breathe, that the price to be paid in exchange is very high. In speaking of the price to be paid, I am not thinking so much of the inevitable side effects which accompany every action as of the deeper problem which is involved: the restriction to what is observable and by repeated experiment falsifiable presupposes the renunciation of real decisions of value, indeed, of the question of truth. I am not affirming that such a restriction would refuse these things their proper place but only that they cannot occur in its own procedure. But because this procedure is the way to success, it is tempting to draw the fallacious conclusion that only what it admits as certain is reasonable and that only what is thus recognized as reasonable enjoys the right to exist. Hence, it is not the method as such but rather the overpowering fascination of its success which thus threatens to lead to the destruction of man. This accounts for the fact that the unification of technical civilization has caused the fragmentation of the philosophical consciousness and the dissolution of its specific content, namely, the question of truth. There are two ways out of this situation, though they are in reality one. First, philosophy can attempt to become wholly "positive" itself. In so doing, however, it has revoked its own charter as philosophy; as a result, the question of truth is abandoned as unscientific by the very university which it once brought forth. But because in the long run pure positivism is unlivable, a second exit suggests itself: truth is not the measure but the product of man. It is replaced by practical results. It too can now be produced "scientifically", for it lies in praxis which creates the future. Truth becomes a method developed as a means of shaping the future. The consequent situation of the individual Christian has been described to a turn by Albert Görres: "I select the cocktail of plausibilities which tastes best to me. Christians secure in their faith often seem to themselves and to others to be overbearing megalomaniacs affected by an infallibility complex."[5] Once pluralism is conceived in such a way, the idea of a magisterium becomes pure absurdity and arrogant pretense. In my opinion, the vehemence with which every kind of magisterial intervention is attacked today depends in large measure on this mental attitude. The claim to be able to state a universal and, therefore, binding truth appears as abstruse "medieval" arrogance. But it could be that even deeper spiritual layers are in play. The suspicion that perhaps there really might be a truth which can be known and which thus represents a claim on me has the force of a personal offense, indeed, of a dangerous attack on the lifestyle in which I have

---

[5] A. Görres, "Glaubensgewißheit in einer pluralistischen Welt", in: *IKZ* 12 (1983): 117–32; citation on 119.

comfortably installed myself; such an attack must be resisted with all the passion which is aroused when one feels oneself struck in the deepest core of one's existence.

Be that as it may, what has been said does not yet complete the panorama of the issues. For so far we have spoken only of the crisis of philosophy; we noted that it is also a crisis of the university and that as such it is a crisis of contemporary civilization, inasmuch as the university is entrusted with the question truth and, in consequence, with the question of man's existence. How, on the other hand, do things stand with theology? I have found a graphic illustration of this problem in the autobiographical sketches of Romano Guardini, who is surely a reliable source. Here Guardini depicts his arduous path to the doctorate and to academic professorship, which proved so difficult for him because German theology had submitted itself unreservedly to the methodological canon of the university, where only history and the natural sciences counted as science. Scientific theology was accordingly reduced to historical theology. Guardini, in contrast, did not wish to become a historian but a theologian and philosopher. In other words, he did not desire to find out what was once the case in the past but rather what is true in the past and in the present and is therefore of concern to us. Such being his endeavor, he had no place in the theology judged fit for the doctorate. Because he was conscious of doing something which was nevertheless entirely worthy of the university, he would say that he was working for a university of the future which did not yet exist.[6] As far as I can see, it still does not exist even today, but it ought to exist, and we ought to continue to work for it.

To be sure, a significant transformation has taken place with respect to the theology of the twenties, in which Guardini had to find his way forward. Historical theology is important; I myself have engaged passionately in historical work and would

---

[6] R. Guardini, *Berichte über mein Leben: Autobiographische Schriften*; posthumously edited by F. Henrich (Düsseldorf, 1984), 46.

be happy to do so again. On the other hand, it is evident that it does not exhaust the whole of theology. The reorientation of the idea of truth toward praxis, which occurred under the influence of the Frankfurt school and of the entire neo-Marxist movement, called the old university positivism thoroughly into question. It thus appeared to be an unexpected opportunity for theology to gain at last a new standing in the university and a new relevance in society. Truth is now no longer excluded but produced by a method of praxis. Hence, so-called "practical theology" provides the real starting and end point of the whole framework of theological sciences: the entire edifice of theological disciplines could be understood in corresponding fashion as a part of the struggle for a more human future on the basis of memories preserved in the history of faith. Theology suddenly had a new opportunity to become "scientific" in the most contemporary sense of the term and at the same time wholly concrete. It goes without saying that this was and is an exciting proposal. And it is this alone which also accounts for what in itself is wholly incomprehensible, namely, that overnight theologians and their communities became the most effective representatives of the neo-Marxist movement. It also explains the passion with which the scientific character of Marxism and its consequent indispensability were asserted. After all, if Marxism were not scientific, this opportunity would collapse in on itself. There is a curious paradox to be noted here. Only Marxism could help an ailing theology back on its feet and restore to it the consciousness of being a real science. On the other hand, only the influx of religious passion and hope could once more lend Marxism, which was already scientifically and politically exhausted, the luster of a bright prospect for humanity outside of its sphere of hegemony. And if the blind leads the blind, both shall fall into the ditch.[7]

---

[7] Though this text was composed in 1985, the intervening collapse of the Marxist system has rendered obsolete only certain accidental details. The fun-

At this point we are confronted afresh with the problem of pluralism. In the last analysis, the concept of a theology in which praxis has succeeded to the truth makes no provision for pluralism at all, just as little, in fact, as does the Marxist conception itself. Hence, a well-known exponent of liberation theology has recently made a telling addition to the functions of unity which are enumerated in the Letter to the Ephesians. The Letter, in order to specify the bases of Christian unity, says: one Lord, one faith, one baptism, one God and Father of all. The theologian in question added "one option", meaning of course a political option, and, insofar as it is unity in praxis, this option forms the only real unity. Pluralism comes into consideration solely as a transitional phase: as long as the official theology of the Church, which takes its direction from the Creed, remains in force, it is necessary to postulate pluralism in order to secure room for theology oriented by "praxis". When all is said and done, however, there can be only *one* option, that is, only *one* praxis and, consequently, only *one* theory to serve it as well. In the long run, the renunciation of truth has no power to liberate. On the contrary, its final result is uniformity. After the evil spirit of a narrow Scholastic orthodoxy has been driven out, in the end seven much more wicked spirits return in its place.

That said, something like a preliminary conclusion of our considerations gradually emerges in outline. From the very beginning it was a constitutive element of the Christian faith that its teaching appealed to man in terms of his ultimate bond, his bond to the truth. In this respect, the social organization arising from faith distinguishes itself from all other associa-

---

damental conviction that praxis is the primary value and that it is possible to produce a better future has remained unshaken by events, even though its conceptual repertory has fallen into disarray. Meanwhile, the idea that this is the basis for the reconciliation of the religions, which are supposed to find common ground in the struggle for a better inner-worldly future, is noticeably spreading.

tions. But precisely because faith penetrates to the level of this bond, it emancipates man in the various domains lying farther in the foreground of his existence. Here there is a relationship to Laski's model: faith orients man at the deepest level, but it does not prescribe to him his individual social roles. For this reason, the Church is not a state, and Christians can live in diverse forms of state and in diverse social groupings. This does not imply any freedom from obligations, any retreat into pure interiority, any abdication of the Christian's social responsibility. Faith is by all means an "option", to which the Decalogue, interpreted in the light of the New Testament, gives very definite contours. It is an option for the equal right of all men and therefore for the inviolability of right by power. It is an option for the unconditional authority of the truth and of man's bond to the truth. It is an option for marital fidelity and for the family as the basic cell of society. It is an option for the sacredness of human life and for the right to life. Hence, it was from the earliest beginning an option for the disenfranchised and oppressed or, as the Bible expresses it, for the widows, the orphans and the sojourners. In this sense it contains unequivocal political and social imperatives which will repeatedly bring Christians into conflict with the powers that be. Yet this does not make it a political recipe, and the Church, therefore, cannot and must not become a political party. Since she must contest the total claim of the political realm, she is also opposed to every analysis which asserts that it is the only one possible and in the same breath that it is the only sure method for producing a healthy society. Such ostensible science is necessarily unscientific, because it presupposes a nonexistent physics of man. If it did exist, man would no longer be man but a machine. Pluralism in the interplay of Church, politics and society is a fundamental value for Christianity. It arose from the teaching of Christianity, which inculcates the relative value of all political and social achievements by shifting theocracy, the consummated form of God's rule and reign, into the eschaton. Consequently, the Church must be sceptical of all political and social mono-cultures. The freedom for diverse political and social options is an interest of the faith itself, just as the distinction between Church and state, the freedom for the organization of communities within the state and, as a result, freedom of religion all spring from faith's very essence. It goes without saying that there can be situations—without prejudice to what has just been said— which necessitate unity of action among Christians, for example, when one or more of these basic options is at stake. Nonetheless, such unity of action is temporary and does not bestow upon the respective association a general and permanent mandate of the Church. Moreover, its form must be worked out in the practical sphere and cannot be prescribed by the Church, whether it be the hierarchy or any so-called "base".

My thesis, then, would read as follows: Because faith signifies an ultimate bond to God, who is truth, it does indeed furnish man with norms for his concrete action in society, yet the community of believers does not find its center of unity in social or political praxis but only in the authentic binding force of the truth itself. Whenever this bond is dissolved, new constraints arise in its place. "The truth will make you free": the bond to the truth is a release of politics from sacral bonds. In this regard, pluralism is not only compatible with faith but is in conformity with it and, to a certain degree, even necessary for it.

2. Pluralism within the Church

Until now we have been dealing exclusively with the sphere of the Church's relations to the outside, which, however, because of the redefinition of faith as praxis has increasingly become her internal sphere, or rather, threatens to displace it. But now it is time to raise the question about this internal sphere itself. Are dogma and the Magisterium the sole principles, or is there a breathing space of plurality even here? In the light of our reflections up to this point, we must doubtless qualify as erroneous those conceptions which envisage the Church as a state whose pretensions must be curtailed to the greatest possible extent by the formation of countervailing associations and by the rights of the individual. For, unlike the state, to which I belong without my consent prior to joining any association and which, in this sense, is a compulsory corporation, the Church is a voluntary society which is unmistakably characterized by a certain content without which it would be purposeless. We shall have to return to this point. For the time being let us assume that the Church has a content, that she receives her contours from a faith which is defined by content and that, owing to this, she can embrace only those who are willing and able to accept this content as their own. The question remains, therefore, as to what room is allowed for the free movement of thought, action and organization within this basic option. This question was posed already in the early Church, though she did not speak in terms of pluralism but rather coined the notion of *symphonia* in order to express her understanding of the synthesis of unity and multiplicity which exists within the ecclesial community. In the Fathers, as far as I can see, the concept of *symphonia* functions on four levels, with the result that it circumscribes quite comprehensively the plural structure of inner-Church unity.

1. *Symphonia* serves to express the unity of the Old and New Testaments—which is the unity of law and gospel, of prophets and apostles, but also the unity of the diverse writings of the New Testament among themselves.[8] At issue here is the basic form of the expression of truth in the Church, a form which rests upon a structure enriched by manifold tensions. The truth

[8] Cf. Clement of Alexandria, *Stromata* 6, 15 (GCS 2, 495, 6) (The symphony of the law and the prophets); Methodius Olympus, *De libero arbitrio* 1 (GCS [ed. Bonwetsch] 146, 19) (The symphony of prophets and apostles); Eusebius, *Historia ecclesiastica* 6, 31, 3 (MG 20, 592 A) (Symphony of the Gospels among themselves).

of the faith resonates not as a mono-phony but as a sym-phony, not as a homophonic, but as a polyphonic melody composed of the many apparently quite discordant strains in the contrapuntal interplay of law, prophets, Gospels and apostles. The omission of one of the thematic elements of this symphony simplifies the performance but is rejected by the Fathers as heresy, that is, as a reductive selection, because the truth lies only in the whole and in its tensions.

2. The word *symphonia* describes the unity of Christians with one another, the unity which is the very form of the Church. Accordingly, this unity is not simply a homophony but rather reflects the structural form of the expression of truth upon which it is founded. It is therefore said that no empirical factor is a sufficient basis for the Church's unity but that this symphony which is the Church can be arranged only by an other-worldly reality—the Holy Spirit.[9]

3. But faith aspires to a greater unity: it intends not merely to organize the socialization of man into a certain group but to effect his characteristic socialization, which consists in communion with God. The unity of men with God, which at the same time brings about the unity of men with one another, unity with the whole of creation and thus unity between the Creator and the creature, is described as *symphonia*.[10]

4. Man himself is a plural being.[11] He is composed not only

[9] Cf. Athanasius, *Orationes tres adversus Arianos* 3, 23 (MG 26, 372 A) (The Holy Spirit as the ground of reciprocal unity among Christians: like the Father and the Son, we too are united in the one accord and symphony of the Holy Spirit).

[10] These ideas are developed, e.g., by Athanasius, *Epist. de synodis Arimini et Seleuciae*, 48 (MG 26, 780 A) in a polemical key against arianizing tendencies which attempted to describe the unity of the Trinity using the model of symphony. In contrast, Athanasius observes that such notions do not capture the specific element of trinitarian unity, for even the saints and angels are "symphonically united" with God.

[11] Cf., for example, Theodorus Heraclensis, *Frag. in Joa.*, 14, 27 (ed. J. Reuß, TU 89 Berlin, 1966).—The motif is taken up again in H. U. von Balthasar, *Die Wahrheit ist symphonisch: Aspekte des christlichen Pluralismus* (Ein-

of body and soul; he always bears more than two souls within himself and suffers from an inner strife. He is in search of his identity, of an identification, in such a way as to integrate his contrary powers and thereby experience redemption. Oneness with himself, which man cannot obtain on his own but must receive from elsewhere—from the one who is more intimate to him than he himself—is likewise described as *symphonia*. This does not obliterate the plurality of dimensions in man's being but forms it from strife into a unity.

A thoroughgoing treatment of the subject which is not content with superficial pragmatisms would have to explore these diverse levels in order to find light for the practical problems involved. Since this would exceed the thematic parameters which it is our task to reflect upon here, I would like to limit myself to submitting a few observations concerning two particular issues which occupy the foreground of attention today. While treating these points, we should naturally not lose sight of the broader context which my mention of the patristic view of our question was meant to include in the discussion, at least by way of allusion.

a. The universal Church and the particular churches

Since the Second Vatican Council, we have once again become clearly aware that the Church cannot be likened to a centrally governed state whose provinces are mere subdivisions of a single administrative apparatus. The eucharistic ecclesiology which streamed back into the Catholic consciousness from Orthodox theology has made it plain that the Church is not formed by a government—in that case she would be a sort of state or association on a par with any other. She is brought forth by the call of Christ, that is, she is formed out of the sacrament and is therefore herself a sacrament. It is the Eucharist, as

siedeln, 1972) [H. U. von Balthasar, *Truth Is Symphonic: Aspects of Christian Pluralism* (San Francisco, 1987)].

Christ's presence and sacrament, which builds up the Church. Consequently, the Church is present as a whole wherever he is, hence, wherever the Eucharist is rightly celebrated. It follows that just as Christ is not half but wholly present, the Church is wholly present wherever he is. On that account, the local churches have the whole reality of the Church, not merely a parcel cut out of the whole. On the other hand, the fresh discovery that Christ can exist only as a whole must not lead us to forget the complementary truth that he can only be one and that we accordingly possess him in his entirety only when we possess him together with others, when we possess him in unity. The unity of the universal Church is in this sense an inner moment of the local church, just as the multiplicity and inherent dignity of the local churches is an essential component of ecclesiastical unity. In what concerns the Church's constitution, this finds expression in the mutual ordination of primacy and episcopacy. The symphony of the one Church in the many churches hangs on the right coordination of the two elements. Seeing that the contours of the problem are so manifold that it is impossible to describe them here even approximately, I would like to content myself with two remarks on this point.[12]

1. The mutual ordination of episcopacy and primacy conceals an even more fundamental principle of the Church's constitution: the mutual implication of the personal and the community dimensions. Monocracy, the sole rule of one person, is always dangerous. Even when the person in question acts out of great ethical responsibility, he can stray into unilateral positions and become rigid. The evolution of government in the modern era has generally struggled more and more toward collegial organs equipped with reciprocal checks and balances. However, the more experiences of such governmental structures accumulate,

---

[12] Cf. the document concerning certain aspects of the understanding of the Church as communio published in 1992; in addition, J. Ratzinger, *Zur Gemeinschaft gerufen* (Freiburg, 1991).

the more clearly perceptible also become the limitation and the risk which they entail: responsibility now slips into anonymity. In the end, no one has to answer for what is done, because it is the group that has decided, and everyone knows that he is not wholly identical with the group. The group levels decisions and takes them out of the hands of individuals. Majorities are products of chance and are too unstable to be the ultimate source of rights. For this reason, the constitution of the Church provides for a harmonious cooperation between the principle of community and the principle of personal responsibility at every level, even though there is a wide difference in juridical character from level to level. The parish priest is linked to his community; the bishop to his presbytery and to his fellow bishops; the Pope to the communion of the bishops. At the same time, there is a final personal responsibility which cannot be waived, substituted or dissolved into any collective, whether at the level of the parish, of the diocese or of the universal Church. That structure of Church government which used formerly to be called the monarchical episcopate should rather be termed the principle of personal responsibility. The Church becomes tangible and answerable in persons; these persons cannot make decisions arbitrarily but only insofar as they are bound in conscience to the faith of the universal Church. Since the Church is a communion which stands on conscience, for purposes of government she can legitimately requisition conscience in order to establish a bond between the community and individual persons.[13] The papal primacy has no real place if it finds no counterpart on the preceding levels—the personal responsibility of a bishop, which this latter cannot delegate to a conference, however important this institution may be to concretize his link to the whole body. Conversely, the episcopal principle is nullified if there is noth-

---

[13] For a more detailed treatment, see my piece "Gewissen und Wahrheit", in: M. Kessler, W. Pannenberg and H. J. Pottmeyer, eds., *Fides Quærens Intellectum: Beiträge zur Fundamentaltheologie. Festschrift für Max Seckler zum 65. Geburtstag* (1992), 293–309.

ing on the level of the Church universal which corresponds to its significance for the particular church. It is precisely this personalistic approach to right and responsibility which results in a variegated and lively pluralism. In fact, the college of bishops is a body composed of those who bear an ultimate personal responsibility for the particular church, which is herself wholly church and in which they embody the responsibility of the universal Church. Only in this way can the episcopal college form a group filled with vitality which reflects the multiplicity of the Spirit in the one Church.

2. At the same time, however, there is a curious reversal of movements. For whereas the papacy appears at first sight to be the guarantor of unity—that every particular church is in truth the one Church—historically speaking, the coexistence of structures relative to the local churches and to the universal Church has proved to be an engine of pluralism. The classic example is the thirteenth-century controversy over the mendicant orders. In the previous period, traditional monasticism had managed to integrate itself without friction into the episcopal order of the Church, because as a rule individual monasteries confined themselves to their own territory and did not interfere in the actual apostolic work entailed in pastoral care. Now, on the contrary, new pastoral movements were suddenly appearing on the scene. Fanning out from one central location, they worked dynamically across the entire European continent and, by preaching, hearing confessions and celebrating the liturgy, entered into direct competition with normal pastoral work. The battle of the secular clergy against the mendicant orders in the universities is only the most visible episode of the struggle which arose as a result of these developments, a struggle which was also a transitional phase between the feudal order and modern, more mobile forms of economic life and therefore amounted to a confrontation of different historical epochs. We would by no means be right to side unilaterally and exclusively with the mendicant orders. On the other hand, it is true that they created a new dynamism in a rigidifying system; that they

afforded the universal Church a new chance to be tangibly and actively present as such in the individual local churches; that this instrument enabled the universal Church to operate concretely as such and thereby regain her missionary élan. Pluralism in the form of energetic missionary activity emanating from the universal Church proved to be fruitful as a second force alongside the indigenous pastoral work of the local churches.[14] But the universal Church could be active in the local church, and in this fashion contribute to a pluralistic, though ultimately unified, pastoral effort, only if there was a bond to a concrete, theologically grounded organ of the universal Church, the office of Peter. It seems to me that hitherto still much too little notice and consideration have been given to the fact that the two great impulses behind the development of the doctrine of primacy to its full form originated not so much from an interest in unifying as from the dynamism released by the exigencies of pluralism. The first stimulus was the struggle for the freedom of the Church in the West, hence, for the distinction between Church and state in their typically Western nonidentity.[15] The impulse came from the "base movements" (so to say) at the level of the whole Church; they fructified and supplemented local pastoral care with the apostolic dynamism of the Church universal. Both facts constitute a sort of practical verification of the Petrine office drawn from the Church's historical expe-

[14] On the historical questions addressed here, see J. Ratzinger, *Das neue Volk Gottes* (Düsseldorf, 1969), 49–71; Y. Congar, "Aspects ecclésiologiques de la querelle entre mendiants et séculiers dans la seconde moitié du XIIIe siècle et le début du XIVe", in: *AHD* 28 (1961): 35–151.

[15] I am alluding here to the basic motif of the Gregorian Reform, which, however, merely continues and concretizes a fundamental theme anchored in the whole tradition of the primacy; cf. the relevant documentation adduced by H. Rahner, *Kirche und Staat im frühen Christentum* (Munich, 1961) [H. Rahner, *Church and State in Early Christianity* (San Francisco, 1992)]. The problem is penetratingly analyzed in E. von Ivánka's important work *Rhomaerreich und Gottesvolk* (Freiburg-Munich 1968). This point is the key to Ivánka's explanation of the difference between the development of Church and culture in the East and in the West.

rience. That both are still of the greatest relevance requires no special demonstration. Only the universal Church is capable of safeguarding the distinction of the particular churches from the state and society. Similarly, we are once again witnessing the phenomenon of apostolic movements "from below" which transcend locality and in which new charisms burst forth to enliven local pastoral work. Today as in the past, such movements, which cannot be reduced to the episcopal principle, find their theological and practical support in the primacy, a proof that it continues to foster living and fruitful pluralism in the Church precisely by making ecclesial unity a concrete reality.

b. Theology and theologies

The questions regarding the structure of the Church which we have just examined in the light of our principal theme point us now toward the content which these structures serve. Until a short time ago, this content seemed to be unambiguously defined, at least in its essential core, by the Creeds, conciliar decisions and dogmas. Today, even this nucleus is called into discussion. Though it is not general practice to contest dogma formally, it is usual to point out that all human speech is culturally conditioned. It is said to be impossible to hand on the faith in definitive formulae. Precisely in order to transmit the identical content, it is supposedly necessary to find constantly new ways of expressing it. This naturally raises a question about the status of Holy Scripture: Supposing this theory to be true, do we have to rewrite the Bible continually as well? Or is not the more correct approach to interpret it unceasingly anew—which, however, implies that we know the Scripture as it is and respect its claim and its inherent inexhaustibility? And just who would be these illuminated spirits able to intuit the enduring content behind all speech despite the absence of any continuity whatsoever in speech itself? Are there really two classes of Christians—the initiated few whose gaze penetrates behind speech and the mass of naïve believers who cling to speech and passively accept whatever new linguistic clothing is served to them without any interest in its connection with the previous one, since this connection is beyond their understanding? Yet did not the Lord pronounce blessed precisely the simple, since they understand God's mysteries better than the learned scribes who seek their own private reality behind the text (cf. Lk 10:21f.)? Logic is not the strong point of such theories: either speech contains no time-transcendent possibility of understanding, in which case it follows that no one can create appropriate new formulae either; or else such a possibility does exist, in which case interpretation is sufficient. Interpretation, however, must justify itself before the given Word and lead back to it, not leave it behind.[16]

I would like to give the floor once again to the psychologist Albert Görres, who speaks of a "Hinduization" of the faith, "in which faith propositions no longer matter because the important thing is contact with a spiritual atmosphere which leads beyond everything that can be said."[17] By way of contrast, Görres expresses in no uncertain terms the historical physiognomy of the Christian faith: "The answer, which has been held faithfully in every epoch, sounds rather different. It affirms that there is no Christianity without a 'laconic streak'. There is no doctrine of Jesus without a skeleton, without dogmatic principle. Jesus had no intention of producing some contentless state of exaltation. . . . His message is a definite one. . . . He does not agree with everyone. . . ."[18] "Catholic Christians believe that the faith is a contoured reality and that it is vitally necessary that it be so, for otherwise it would be robbed of meaning. . . . They believe that the Church is able to—and should—see to it that these contours are 'catholic' in the literal sense, hence, that at all times they manifest the *whole* of revela-

---

[16] I have dealt with these questions in somewhat greater detail in debate with K. Rahner in my *Theologischen Prinzipienlehre* (Munich, 1982), 127–39 [J. Ratzinger, *Principles of Catholic Theology* (San Francisco, 1989), 122–33].

[17] Görres, 129.

[18] Ibid.

tion without narrowing and distortion. . . ."[19] In reality, faith heals and strengthens to the extent that it opens knowledge to man—true knowledge, otherwise, it would be no knowledge at all. It tells him what he himself can perhaps glimpse from afar but which no human being can secure for him: the truth about the origin and goal of his own being. It furnishes him with a knowledge which alone makes sense of everything else which he knows. To remove from faith its claim to truth, to stated, understandable truth, is an example of that false modesty which is diametrically opposed to humility because it refuses to accept the *condition humaine*; it is a renunciation of that dignity of being a man which makes human suffering bearable and endows it with greatness.[20]

If this is granted, it follows that faith establishes specifiable dogmatic reference points. It follows that even the simple—perhaps they in particular—can possess the right faith and that they can have it in every age. If the possibility of indicating the essentials of the faith "without distortion" is necessary to

---

[19] Ibid., 130.

[20] From today's perspective, the significance of the work of R. Guardini seems to me to reside principally in the resoluteness with which he asserts against every historicism and pragmatism man's capacity for truth and the orientation of philosophy and theology to truth. In some sense, his entire thinking and striving are summed up in a journal entry of February 28, 1954: "Truth has such a clear and calm power. My aim in pastoral work is this: to help by the power of the truth" (*Wahrheit des Denkens und Wahrheit des Tuns*, ed. by J. Messerschmid, 3d ed. [Paderborn, 1980], 85). Guardini's last published statement, the address delivered on the occasion of his eighty-fourth birthday, is another powerful treatment of the theme of truth and could be considered as a kind of spiritual testament. Using Plato, he makes explicit the knowledge of man's incommensurability with the truth. In reality, man must appear foolish to himself when he risks speaking of the truth yet has no choice but to expose himself to this risk—and he must do so precisely in the recognition of his own absurdity. Only the presence of both elements, that is, the courage to search for the truth and the humility to accept one's ridiculousness, enables man to maintain the right mean between truthless cynicism and self-righteous fanaticism. This important text is to be found in: R. Guardini, *Stationen und Rückblicke* (Würzburg, 1965), 41–50.

the faith itself, then there must be an authority able to exercise this function. In consequence, the Church herself must have a voice; she must be capable of expressing herself as Church and of distinguishing false belief from the true faith. This implies that faith and theology are not identical and that each has its own characteristic voice but that the voice of theology is dependent upon that of faith and oriented toward it. Theology is interpretation and must remain such. When it no longer interprets but, so to speak, lays hands on the substance of the faith and alters it by inventing a new text for itself, it ceases to be theology. After all, it no longer interprets but speaks in its own name. The result may then be termed philosophy of religion and prove interesting as such, but it enjoys no basis and authority beyond the private reflection of whoever happens to be speaking. Faith and theology differ in the same way as text and interpretation. Unity rests in faith, while theology is the domain of plurality. To that extent, the very act of fixing the common reference point—faith—makes plurality in theology possible.

We must still determine the two sides of this relationship somewhat more precisely. We have observed that definiteness about its tenets is an integral part of faith, that this definiteness implies the possibility of expressing the faith and that this, in turn, requires an authority competent to do so. We drew from this the further conclusion that the Church as such cannot be dumb but must have the gift of speech, that is, she must be able to state what is essential to her. This brings us to a decisively important aspect of the act of faith. The faith of the Church does not exist as an ensemble of texts, rather, the texts—the words—exist because there is a corresponding subject which gives them their basis and their inner coherence. Empirically speaking, the preaching of the apostles called into existence the social organization "Church" as a kind of single historical subject. One becomes a believer by joining this community of tradition, thought and life, by living personally from its continuity of life throughout history and by acquiring a share in its way of understanding, its speech and its thought. For the believer, however, this Church is not just any sociological subject but a truly new subject called into being by the Holy Spirit, which precisely for that reason throws open the impassable frontiers of human subjectivity, putting man in contact with the ground of reality itself.[21] By its very nature, faith is believing communion with the whole Church. The "I believe" of the Creed refers, not to some private "I", but rather to the corporate "I" of the Church. Faith is possible in the measure that I become one with this corporate "I", which does not abolish my own "I" but broadens it out and, in this way, brings it to itself for the first time.

This observation is important because it leads us past all words and formulae into a realm lying before and beyond speech. The human words in which faith is expressed never wholly capture their content, which reaches into eternity— such is the kernel of truth in those theories which in their extreme form amount to a "Hinduizing" of the Christian faith. The speech of faith is no mathematical language, which is the only univocal language there is. The deeper human words penetrate into the essence of reality, the more insufficient they become. All of this emerges more clearly if we turn our attention to the concrete evidence of the language of faith, which is characterized by two immediately obvious facts. First, this speech consists of images, not concepts. Second, it presents itself in a historical succession of statements. In this regard, the basic tension between the Old and New Testaments al-

[21] Cf. H. de Lubac, *La Foi chrétienne: Essai sur la structure du Symbole des Apôtres* (Paris, 1970) [H. de Lubac, *The Christian Faith: An Essay on the Structure of the Apostles' Creed* (San Francisco, 1986)]; Internationale Theologenkommission, *Pluralismus*, 36–42. In his "probation lecture" held at Bonn in 1922, R. Guardini had already stated programmatically that theology presupposes the corporate subject "Church" in order to maintain its identity: "Anselm von Canterbury und das Wesen der Theologie"; published in his volume of essays: *Auf dem Wege: Versuche* (Mainz, 1923). Another very illuminating work on this subject is L. Bouyer, *Le Métier du théologien. Entretiens avec G. Daix* (Paris, 1979).

ready indicates to what an extent the truth of faith can become accessible in language only within the inner coherence of the whole, and not in separate propositions. If one strikes out the continuity of a subject which organically traverses the whole of history and which remains one with itself throughout its own transformations, nothing is left beyond contradictory speech fragments which cannot subsequently be brought into any relation. The tendency to search for what is most ancient and original behind present developments is the logical conclusion of the loss of the binding element which holds history together and unifies it in the midst of its contradictions. Theology becomes archeology and busies itself with exhuming the authentic ideal behind what really appears before our eyes as Christianity. Such reconstructed Christianity, however, is always a selective Christianity, which loses the tension and the wealth of the whole. The disjointed pluralism of subjectively minted selective Christianities comes to replace the inner plurality of the symphony of the faith.

We are obliged to say, therefore, that this disintegrative pluralism arises when men no longer feel themselves equal to the arc of tensions inherent in the whole of the faith. It always presupposes a previous narrowing and impoverishment, which are not reversed by the proliferation of juxtaposed partial Christianities rising and falling in succession—on the contrary, this merely brings fully to light the penury of every solitary effort. In contrast, fruitful theological pluralism succeeds in bringing the pluriform historical manifestations of faith into unity. Such unity, far from cancelling multiplicity, is the recognition that it is the organic structure of the truth which transcends man. To be sure, there is a persistent suspicion today, even among wholly Church-minded theologians, that orthodox theology is hopelessly condemned merely to repeat magisterial statements of doctrine and traditional formulae. The space for thought seems to be crammed with such an immense clutter of old and new decisions that at every step one inevitably stumbles against some definition, and there is simply no more air to

breathe freely. To become "creative", it appears downright indispensable to throw out the old rubbish and to pass boldly
even to open contradiction.

But what certainty is really left for such creativity to start
from? Are personal plausibility and harmonious accord with
a portion of the *Zeitgeist* a truly secure foundation? When a
doctor errs and, instead of patiently accommodating himself
to the laws of anatomy and of life, risks a "creative" idea, the
consequences are readily apparent. Although the damage is not
so immediately noticeable in the case of a theologian, in reality even here too much is at stake for him to trust himself
simply to his momentary conviction, for he is dealing with a
matter which affects man and his future and in which every
failed intervention has its consequences. Certainly, it is easier
to clear one's path of the cumbersome furniture of dogma and
to abandon oneself to plausibility than to remain at a standstill
before a reality which obstructs the way and to make oneself
vulnerable to its demands. At this stage, it is helpful to cast a
side glance at natural science. It has achieved its great successes
thanks, not to a free-floating creativity, but to the strictest ad-
hesion to its object. Naturally, it must constantly probe the
object on all sides with anticipatory hypotheses and seek new
methods of penetrating it with questions which will elicit answers. Once given, however, none of the answers can simply be cleared away. On the contrary, the more they increase
in number, the more possibilities of inquiry are disclosed and
the more concrete space is won for real creativity. I mean the
sort of creativity which does not forge ahead into the void but
connects the already existing paths in order to open up new
ones. It is not otherwise in theology. It is precisely this pro-
fusion of the forms of faith in the unity of the Old and New
Testaments, of the New Testament and early Church dogma,
of all these elements together and the ongoing life of faith,
which increases the excitement and fecundity of inquiry. To
seek the inner unity and totality of the truth in the grand historical structure of the faith, with its abundant contrasts, is

more stimulating and productive than to cut the knots and to assert that this unity does not exist. In the confrontation with earlier expressions of faith, which are seemingly remote from us, the present is left richer than if it remains in splendid isolation. There are, of course, many petty minds and repeaters of the past even among orthodox theologians. They are to be found everywhere; hack theology has enjoyed a particularly rapid growth precisely where there was too much noisy chatter about creativity. For a long time I shared the impression that the so-called heretics were really more interesting than theologians of the Church, at least in more recent times. Now, however, when I consider the great believing teachers from Möhler to Newman and Scheeben, from Rosmini to Guardini, or in our day de Lubac, Congar, Balthasar—how much richer and more relevant is their testimony than the witness of those who let the corporate subject Church slip through their fingers. These masters are a clear witness of another truth: pluralism happens, not when we make it the object of our desire, but when everyone wants the truth with all his power and in his own epoch. But to desire it requires that, instead of making ourselves the measure, we accept as the voice and the way of the truth the greater understanding which is already present as a prior given in the Church's faith. I believe, moreover, that this same law also applies to the new guiding models of theology which are sought today: African, Latin American, Asian theology, and so on. The great French theology was born, not because theologians wished to do something French, but because they expected nothing less from themselves than to find the truth and to express it as adequately as possible. For that reason it proved to be both French and universal. The same is true of the great theology of Italy, Germany and Spain. It is perennially true. Only freedom from ulterior motives is fruitful. And, in reality, we have not reached the pinnacle by having affirmed *ourselves*, set forth *ourselves* and raised a monument to *ourselves*—we have attained it when we have drawn closer to the truth. The truth is never monotonous, nor is it ever exhausted in a single form, because our mind beholds it only in fragments; yet at the same time it is the power which unifies us. And only pluralism in relation to unity is great.

PART 3

APPLICATIONS

On the "Instruction concerning the Ecclesial Vocation of the Theologian"

Prefatory Note

On May 24, 1990, the Congregation for the Doctrine of the Faith published an "Instruction" on the ecclesial vocation of the theologian which touched off an unexpectedly passionate debate. The first part of this chapter reprints the text with which I presented the document to the press when it was first issued. I believe that this text is still suited to explain the structure and purpose of the document without resorting to polemics. In the second part, I attempt to respond to a few of the weightier objections against the Instruction, in order to pursue the dialogue which began—though for the most part in a very negative tone —with its publication.

1. Presentation

The significance of the theologian and of theology for the whole community of believers became evident in a new way at the Second Vatican Council. Before the Council, it had been usual to consider theology as a pursuit reserved to a small circle of clerics, as an elitist and abstract affair which could hardly lay claim to the interest of the Church at large. The new mode of seeing and expressing the faith which prevailed at the Council was the fruit of the dramatic, and until then practically unnoticed, history of a new theological sensibility which had made its debut after the First World War in conjunction with new spiritual movements. The regnant mood of liberalism, with its naïve faith in progress, had collapsed in the horror of the war, carrying with it theological Modernism, which had attempted to assimilate faith to the liberal worldview. The liturgical movement, the biblical and ecumenical movements, finally, a strong Marian movement shaped a new spiritual climate favorable to the growth of a new theology, which later bore fruit for the whole Church at the Second Vatican Council. The bishops themselves were surprised by the bounty of a theology which in part was still unfamiliar to them and willingly took the theologians as teachers and guides into hitherto virgin territory, even though the final decisions regarding what could be adopted as an official expression of the Council and, therefore, of the Church herself, remained in the hands of the Fathers.

After the Council, the dynamic of this development continued apace. Theologians increasingly felt themselves to be the true teachers of the Church and even of the bishops. Moreover, since the Council they had been discovered by the mass media and had captured their interest. The Magisterium of the Holy See now appeared in the public eye to be the last holdover of a failed authoritarianism. The impression was that the insistent claim to competence on the part of a nonacademic authority threatened to keep thought under tutelage, whereas in reality the path to knowledge could not be prescribed by authority but rather depended solely upon the force of argument. In these circumstances, it has become necessary to reflect anew on the position of theology and of the theologian as well as on their relationship to the Magisterium. Such a reflection would attempt to understand both theology and the Magisterium in accord with their inner logic and, in so doing, would contribute not only to peace in the Church but, above all, to a correct way of relating faith and reason.

It is this task which the Instruction tries to serve. Hence, it is ultimately concerned with an anthropological problem: if religion and reason cannot be brought into the proper correspondence, man's spiritual life disintegrates into a flat rationalism dominated by technique, on the one hand, and into a dark irrationalism, on the other. The wave of esotericism which we are witnessing today is an indication that the deeper layers of man's being can no longer be integrated into the predominant positivistic rationalism and that, in consequence, atavistic forms of superstition are once more gaining power over him. Positivism contests man's capacity for truth, for it holds that his knowledge is restricted to the producible and verifiable; meanwhile, irrational forces triumph outside the domain of production. Man, though seemingly totally liberated, becomes the servant of inscrutable powers. For this reason, the Instruction places the subject of theology within the broad horizon of the question of man's capacity for truth and of his true freedom. The Christian faith is not a pastime, and the Church is not one club among others of a similar or even of a different sort. Rather, faith responds to the primordial question of man regarding his origin and goal. It bears on those basic problems which Kant characterized as the essential core of philosophy: What can I know? What may I hope for? What is man? In other words, faith has to do with truth, and only if man is capable of truth can it also be said that he is called to freedom.

The first item in the alphabet of faith is the statement: In the beginning was the Word. Faith reveals to us that eternal reason is the ground of all things or, put in other terms, that things are reasonable from the ground up. Faith does not aim to offer man some sort of psychotherapy; *its* psychotherapy is the truth. This is what makes it universal and by nature missionary. It is also the reason why faith is intrinsically "*quærens intellectum*", as the Fathers say, that is, in search of understanding. Understanding, hence, rational engagement with the priorly given Word, is a constitutive principle of the Christian faith, which of necessity spawns theology. This trait, moreover, distinguishes the Christian faith from all other religions, even from a purely historical point of view. Theology is a specifically Christian phenomenon which follows from the structure of this faith.

But what distinguishes theology from the philosophy of religion and from secular religious science? The answer is that man's reason knows that it has not been left to its own devices. It is preceded by a Word which, though logical and rational, does not originate from reason itself but has been granted it as a gift and, as such, always transcends it. It remains a task which we never completely fulfill in history. Theology is pondering what God has said and thought before us. If it abandons this secure ground, it annuls its own constitution. There is then no way to avoid sinking into scepticism and letting existence split apart into rationalism and irrationalism.

Let us return to our Instruction. It treats of the task of the theologian in this broad context and thereby manifests plainly the greatness of his mission. A striking feature of the division of the text is that it does not begin with the Magisterium but with the truth, which it presents as a gift of God to his people. The truth of faith, in fact, is not bestowed upon the isolated individual, for God has willed instead to build history and community with it. It has its place in a common subject: the people of God, the Church. The vocation of the theologian is presented next, and the Magisterium and the mutual relation of the two are discussed only afterward. This implies two things:

a. Theology is not simply and exclusively an ancillary function of the Magisterium: it is not limited to gathering arguments for a priori magisterial decisions. If that were so, the Magisterium and theology would draw perilously close to an ideology whose sole interest is the acquisition and preservation of power. Theology has a specific origin of its own. The document, borrowing from Saint Bonaventure, designates two roots of theology in the Church. The first is the dynamism toward truth and understanding inherent in the faith; the second is the dynamism of love, which desires to know the beloved more intimately. Correspondingly, there are two directions in theology, which, however, continually cross and recross each other. The first, more outwardly moving direction devotes its efforts to dialogue with every reasonable search for truth; the second, which moves predominantly inward, strives to fathom the inner logic and depth of the faith.

b. The document treats the ecclesial mission of the theologian, not in the context of the dualism Magisterium-theology, but rather in the framework of the triangular relationship de-

fined by the people of God, understood as the bearer of the
sensus fidei and the common locus of all faith, the Magisterium
and theology. The development of dogma in the last 150 years
is a clear index of how closely these three elements hang together: the dogmas of 1854, 1870 and 1950 became possible
because the *sensus fidei* had discovered them, while the Magisterium and theology followed its lead and tried slowly to catch
up with it.

   This is already a statement of the essentially ecclesial identity
of theology. Theology is never simply the private idea of one
theologian. If it were, it could count for little, for as a private
idea it would sink rapidly into insignificance. On the contrary,
the Church, as a living subject which endures amid the changes
of history, is the vital milieu of the theologian; the Church pre-
serves faith's experiences with God. Theology can remain historically relevant only if it acknowledges this living environment, inserts itself into it and attains an inner participation in
it. It follows that the Church is not an organization which the
theologian must regard as alien and extrinsic to thought. Insofar as the Church is a corporate subject which transcends the
narrowness of individuals, she is the condition which makes
theological activity possible. It is thus evident that two things
are essential for the theologian. First, the methodological rigor
which is part and parcel of the business of scholarship; in this
regard, the document refers to philosophy, the historical disciplines and the human sciences as privileged partners of the
theologian. But he also has need of inner participation in the
organic structure of the Church; he needs that faith which is
prayer, contemplation and life. Only in this symphony does
theology come into being.

   This also makes for an organic understanding of the Magisterium. We said that the Church enters into the nature of
theology. But the Church is more than an exterior organization of believers only if she has her own voice. Faith precedes
theology; theology is the quest to understand the Word which,
not having been devised by us, elicits the utmost effort from

our thought but is never engulfed by it. This Word which precedes theological research is the measure of theology and requires its own organ—the Magisterium, which Christ committed to the apostles and, through them, to their successors. I do not wish to discuss in detail here how the document explains the relationship between the Magisterium and theology. Under the title "reciprocal collaboration", it sets forth the task proper to each and explains how they ought to live and work together. The priority of faith, which lends the Magisterium authority and a final right of decision, does not obliterate the independence of theological research but guarantees it a solid basis. The document does not conceal the fact that there can be tensions even under the most favorable circumstances. These tensions, however, can be productive, provided that each side sustains them in the recognition that its function is intrinsically ordered to that of the other. The text also presents the various forms of binding authority which correspond to the grades of the Magisterium. It states—perhaps for the first time with such candor—that there are magisterial decisions which cannot be the final word on a given matter as such but, despite the permanent value of their principles, are chiefly also a signal for pastoral prudence, a sort of provisional policy. Their kernel remains valid, but the particulars determined by circumstances can stand in need of correction. In this connection, one will probably call to mind both the pontifical statements of the last century regarding freedom of religion and the anti-Modernist decisions of the beginning of this century, especially the decisions of the then Biblical Commission. As warning calls against rash and superficial accommodations, they remain perfectly legitimate: no less a personage than J. B. Metz, for example, has remarked that the anti-Modernist decisions of the Church performed the great service of saving her from foundering in the bourgeois-liberal world. Nevertheless, with respect to particular aspects of their content, they were superseded after having fulfilled their pastoral function in the situation of the time.

In contrast to these healthy forms of tension, a defective variety is treated in the second part of the final chapter under the heading "dissent", wherewith the Instruction avails itself of a catchword which came into vogue in the United States in the 1960s. When theology organizes itself according to the principle of majority rule and constructs a countermagisterium which offers the faithful alternative modes of behavior, it misses its own essence. It sets itself up as a political factor, utilizes channels of power to represent its interests and appeals to the political model of majority. By disavowing the Magisterium, it forfeits the firm ground under its feet and, by stepping out of the realm of thought into the play of power, it also falsifies its scientific character. It thus loses the two foundations of its existence.

The Instruction was published in the hope that the distinction between constructive kinds of tension and a perverse and unacceptable form of antithesis between theology and the Magisterium will help to relax the strained atmosphere in the Church. The Church needs a sound theology. Theology needs the living voice of the Magisterium. May the Instruction contribute to a renewal of dialogue between the Magisterium and theology and thereby be of service to the Church at the close of this second millennium and, with her, to humanity in its struggle for truth and freedom.

2. Toward a Discussion of the Text

The Instruction briefly presented here has kindled a controversy, which in part has proceeded in a vehement tone. It has been shown that the Instruction aimed to call attention to the specific role of theology in the Church and thus to the particular responsibility of the theologian. Yet theologians, especially in German-speaking Countries, together with a group of Latin American theologians, claimed to see in the text the precise opposite—a constriction of theological inquiry which posed a threat to its authentic nature. The declaration of the "Study Guild of Catholic Dogmaticians and Fundamental Theologians in German-speaking Countries" maintained an even tone and took pains to weigh the issues objectively; the same can be said of the statement of Austrian theologians. Individual scholars like P. Hünermann and D. Mieth, on the other hand, engaged in a fierce polemic.[1] Nor is a commentary undersigned by a good one hundred Latin American theologians exactly delicate in its appraisals when it condemns the text as "incriminatory" and "intellectualistic". The Congregation is charged with repudiating what Rome had supposedly repudiated in the nineteenth century: the people, democracy and public opinion.[2] A comprehensive critical confrontation with these reactions is out of the question here; it is to be hoped that in the theological debate corrective voices capable of leading to a fruitful dialogue beyond the controversies of the moment will gradually also make themselves heard.[3]

Here I wish merely to enter briefly into three problematic areas which call for further reflection. First, however, some obvious misunderstandings in the declaration of the German-language Study Guild ought to be addressed. The German theo-

[1] Cf. the collection of articles edited by P. Hünermann and D. Mieth: *Streitgespräch um Theologie und Lehramt: Die Instruktion über die kirchliche Berufung des Theologen in der Diskussion* (Frankfurt/Main, 1991). I cite the public statement of the German-language Study Guild as it appeared in the *Schweizer Kirchenzeitung* 47 (1990): 673; it is signed by D. Wiederkehr. The statement of representatives of the Austrian faculties of theology was, to my knowledge, not published. A helpful contribution to understanding the Instruction is R. Tremblay, " 'Donum veritatis'. Un document qui donne à penser", in: *Nouvelle revue théologique* 114 (1992): 391–411.

[2] "A Missao eclesial do teólogo: Subsidios de leitura e elementos para um diálogo em torno à 'Instruçao sobre a vocaçao eclesial do teólogo' ", in: *Rev. Eclesiastica Brasileira*, year 50, fascicle 200 (December 1990): 771–807.

[3] This is the drift of the article by M. Seckler, which appears in the volume by Hünermann and Mieth cited above, "Der Dialog zwischen dem Lehramt und den Theologen", 232–40; see in addition the article of R. Tremblay mentioned in n. 1; see further A. Rauscher, "Ständige Kritik tötet die Freude am Glauben", in: *Forum kath. Theol.* 6 (1990): 277–81.

logians, in presenting their fundamental misgiving, assert that
the Instruction envisages the theologian as the mere delegate
of the Magisterium; this is simply false. In fact, number 22 of
the document, which they adduce as evidence on behalf of this
claim, is meant to stress the specific element of the "canonical
mission", or the "authorization to teach". This element is not
identical with the essence of theology as such but rather denotes
a concrete juridical procedure for placing oneself at the service
of the doctrine of the faith. That theology as such is by no means
a mere derivative of the Magisterium is clearly brought out in
the second part of the Instruction—in the description of the
theologian's mission. Conversely, it is quite evident to everyone who reflects without bias that the acceptance of an ecclesiastical commission implies the contraction of a legal obligation
to the teaching Church. No structure peculiar to the Church
is in question here. After all, even the assumption of a state
professorship creates a duty of loyalty toward the state. In connection with this last point, I would like to draw attention to
the remarkable phenomenon that to date it has seemingly not
occurred to any German theologian that the oath of loyalty
to the constitution which is required of those entering upon
state professorships might represent an unreasonable restriction
of scholarly freedom and that it might be incompatible with
a conscience formed by the Sermon on the Mount. How, on
the contrary, the same procedure in the ecclesiastical sphere ex-
ceeds the bounds of all that is tolerable is—for me, at any rate—
impossible to understand. In general, German theologians are
conspicuously friendly toward the state; they obviously see in
it a refuge for freedom, whereas they feel themselves menaced
by the Church—when, for example, it is said that in Germany
the Church's loyalty oath may be administered to professors
employed by the state only with the latter's consent.[4] History

---

[4] So writes the Munich canonist H. Schmitz, as cited by R. Frieling, "In-
strumentalisierte Freiheit der Theologie?", in: *ZThK* (1991), 135ff. Frieling's
article, written in a dispassionate and objective style, says much that is worth

ought to put us on guard against such attempts to court the state's favor. The period of the Evangelical struggle between church and state makes it quite clear that this situation should compel reflection on the limits of the public character of theology and of its obligation to the state.[5]

The statement of the German Study Guild also errs when it introduces an opposition between the Pope's address at Altötting and the Instruction, even though the latter follows the papal text almost literally in affirming that in the case of tensions between the Magisterium and theology which do not call in question the object of faith as such, it is necessary to preserve unity in love.[6] The Instruction goes beyond what was said at Altötting when it speaks of a certain inevitability of tensions and says that they can represent a dynamic element; they can serve as a stimulus for the Magisterium and for theology in the discharge of their respective tasks and in their mutual dialogue.[7] The remark that the Instruction concedes the possibility of error and of an inadequate grasp of the issues only with regard to the past also appears somewhat curious. When it is a question of ascertaining facts, one can speak only of the past; at the same time, to mention the past implies the admission that such events can repeat themselves.

---

consideration but also manifests conspicuously the tendency to disqualify the Church as a "nonscientific" authority in relation to theology, together with willing subordination to the state. In the long run, such a course would necessarily cause Christianity in Germany to sink to the level of a pure *religio civilis*, a situation which would also endanger the freedom of belief.

[5] Cf. E. Wolf, "Kirchenkampf", in: *RGG* 3: 1443–53; interesting comments can be found in the autobiographical memoirs of H. Thielicke, *Zu Gast auf einem schönen Stern* (Hamburg, 1984), esp. 88–138; H. Schlier, "Die Beurteilung des Staates im Neuen Testament", in: idem, *Die Zeit der Kirche*, 2d ed. (Freiburg, 1958; original printing of the text, 1932). Cf. the third chapter of this book, "The Spiritual Basis and Ecclesial Identity of Theology".

[6] Instruction, no. 26.

[7] Instruction, no. 25.

a. Authority only in the case of infallibility?

We come now to questions which demand a somewhat more fundamental reflection. I perceive a first problem, which is moving increasingly into the foreground of the debates, reflected in the remark that the Study Guild makes its own "all those declarations of the Magisterium issued under the prerogative of infallibility, which belongs to the Church as Christ's gift", whereas in all other judgments, the decision would depend on the weight of argument. Initially, this sounds very illuminating, but on closer examination it proves to be quite problematical, since it means for all intents and purposes that doctrinal decisions can exist—if at all—solely in situations where the Church may lay claim to infallibility; outside of this sphere, only argument would hold weight. The result is that there could be no certainty shared by the whole community of the Church. It seems to me that we have before us a typically Western restriction and legalistic reduction of the notion of faith which radicalizes certain one-sided developments which begin to make their appearance around the High Middle Ages. A parallel may render the issue clearer: from about the thirteenth century on, interest in the conditions necessary for validity begins to push every other consideration to the margin of sacramental theology. Increasingly, everything ceases to matter except the alternative between valid and invalid. Those elements which do not affect validity appear to be ultimately trivial and interchangeable. Thus, in the case of the Eucharist, for example, this is expressed in an ever-stronger fixation on the words of consecration; that which is actually constitutive for validity becomes more and more strictly limited. Meanwhile, the eye for the living structure of the Church's liturgy is progressively lost. Everything other than the words of consecration appears to be mere ceremony, which happens to have evolved into its present form but in principle might just as easily have been omitted. The characteristic nature of liturgy and the irreplaceable liturgical sense cease to be regarded as important, falling as they do outside the narrow limits of a legally defined minimalism. But the truth that this juridically necessary factor retains its meaning solely when it remains within the living totality of the liturgy had to be relearned only with great labor. A good part of the liturgical crisis of the Reformation was due to these constrictive tendencies, which are also the key to understanding the liturgical crisis of the present. If today the entire liturgy has become the playground of private "creativity", which can romp at will just as long as the words of consecration are kept in place, at work is the same reduction of vision whose origin lies in an erroneous development typical of the West but quite unthinkable in the Eastern Church.

Let us return from this example to the question before us. As a strictly circumscribed juridical category, infallibility first developed with such rigorous clarity in the Middle Ages, as was demonstrated in the controversy with Küng. We must not conclude, however, that previously everything had been left to argument, that is, to scholarly dispute. No one believed it necessary to reduce the living organism of the doctrine of the faith to the skeleton of infallibility but, on the contrary, saw the essential precisely in the vital figure delineated by the rule of faith and the Creed. Both in doctrine and in liturgy, what really matters is lost when one feels obliged to distill a juristical minimum, beyond which everything is left subject to arbitrariness. Here too we would do well to learn to look once more beyond the fence of Western thinking and to make the attempt to understand anew the original vision which has remained largely intact in the East. Certainly, the knowledge that, under special conditions, the gift of making an infallible pronouncement has been conferred upon the Church cannot and ought not to be withdrawn. This, however, is meaningful only so long as such an act of fixing a limit, an act whose necessity is determined by particular circumstances, is embedded in a vital structure of common certainty in faith. More important than the concept of infallibility is therefore that of *auctoritas*, which, nevertheless, has well-nigh disappeared from our thought. Yet in reality it can never be wholly absent, because it represents a basic presupposition of community life. What would be the result if from now on the state were to enact as a universally binding norm only what can be considered the infallibly correct solution of a given problem? What would happen if the same procedure were mandatory in the economy, in the school or in the family? The crisis of our social organism may be traced, among other causes, to such tendencies and to the misconstrual of democracy as a constant questioning of everything by everyone. States can continue to exist and to be governed only because laws are still regarded as binding (even though subject to revision) when they are issued by the legitimate authority. This comparison limps, of course, because the common teaching of the Church regards other matters than the state's legislation. Yet it is able to show that *auctoritas* cannot be reduced to infallibility. For a community which is based essentially upon common conviction, *auctoritas* is indispensable where its principal tenets are concerned, and precisely an *auctoritas* whose word can mature and become purer through living development.

Let us retain as a conclusion of this reflection that binding authority cannot be the prerogative of infallibility alone. It lies in the living, total form of the faith, which as such must always be capable of new expression lest it disappear in the whirl of changing hypotheses. That *auctoritas* admits of very different degrees is clearly stated in the document and, strictly speaking, should be looked upon, not as an impediment, but as a stimulus to theology. That one degree differs from the others does not imply, however, that lower-ranking *auctoritas* does not rate as *auctoritas* at all. Here once again a new and more differentiated consciousness needs to develop, and the Instruction was intended as a contribution toward that end.

b. The Magisterium, the university and the mass media

Let us proceed to a second question, which comprises two aspects. The first has to do with the position of theology in the university; the second, with ways of arbitrating the fruitful tension between the Magisterium and theology spoken of by the Instruction. I have already alluded in the foregoing to the extremely dubious tendency to play off the state against the Church and to enlist it as a refuge of freedom in opposition to the Church, its alleged menace. This tendency, which in the light of recent history must be labeled as truly absurd, is usually connected with the more subtle argument that the essence of the university cannot be harmonized with the pretensions of the Church's Magisterium; the traditional place of theology in the "house of learning" is endangered by the extension of magisterial claims—so says the Study Guild of German-speaking Fundamental Theologians and Dogmaticians.[8] Now the presence of theology in the university is, in my opinion, a precious patrimony which it is incumbent upon us to defend. That theology be at home in the "house of learning" and be a partner in its discourse is crucially important both for theology and for the other sciences. That theology be able to research and speak with the seriousness and liberty which pertain to scientific endeavor is a value which everyone must have at heart. On the other hand, how long the place of theology in the university can be defended in a society which to an increasing degree defines itself decidedly as agnostic is a question whose gravity we cannot afford to ignore. In fact, theology can remain at home in the university provided that society, despite its fundamental neutrality in worldview, accords to the Christian faith a special role in its own spiritual foundation, that is, does not place it on a level with every other religion or *Weltanschauung*. We do not know whether this will continue to be the case for long.

This, however, is not the question which is to be discussed

[8] 674.

here, though theology must give it serious consideration wherever it is installed in state universities. Here I am concerned with a more far-reaching problem: how, in general, theology ought to define its position as a "science" and, consequently, its status in institutions of learning. It was manifest from the beginning that theology is not some specialized discipline on a par with all others, nor must this fact be glossed over today with the ultimately unreal appearance of a "scientific method", which, in any case, does not exist as a unitary value. The observation of such noted historians as Theodor Mommsen, Jacob Burckhardt and Golo Mann that history cannot be science in the strict sense because its object is not the repeatable but the unrepeatable[9] should be an occasion for theologians as well to give thought to their special variety of "scientific method" and to have the courage to be themselves. Despite every defense of the place of theology in the "house of learning", theology must not forget that it dwells in more than one house. In this regard, a recently published article by G. Alberigo on the development and characteristics of theology as a science deserves our attention.[10] Alberigo demonstrates how at the close of the twelfth century theology rushed as impetuously as a flash flood from its traditional centers—the bishop's residence, the monastery and the chapter of the canons regular—to a new, ecclesiastically neutral center, the university, and in so doing radically altered its spiritual and scientific complexion. Alberigo also shows clearly the inevitability of this process, considering the exhaustion of patristic and monastic theology. He draws out the gain which accrued to theology thanks to this shift, a gain which consisted not least of all in "greater freedom for theological research". But this well-known historian also brings to light the reverse side of this "dislocation" of teaching (and

[9] Cf. J. Fest, *Wege zur Geschichte. Über T. Mommsen, J. Burckhardt und G. Mann* (Zurich, 1992); for example, 25; 81; 130.

[10] G. Alberigo, "Sviluppo e caratteri della teologia come scienza", in: *Cristianesimo nella storia* 11 (1990): 257–74.

inquiry), which led away from "the most vital centers of the Church", the diocese and the monastery, and thus signified a removal from the pastoral and spiritual context of local church realities. The orientation of theology toward a scientific status initiated a movement tending to divorce theology from the life of the Church: an ever more pronounced "hiatus develops between the Christian community and the institutional Church herself, on the one hand, and the guild of theologians, on the other. The fact that the university became the new seat of research and of the teaching of theology without a doubt enervated its ecclesial dynamism and furthermore severed theology from vital contact with spiritual experiences."[11] Yet another important consequence comes into view: the intensity of the change which had taken place distanced Christian thought drastically from the pattern of the first millennium and from Oriental and Greek culture. "Scientific theology soon found itself Western and Latin, far beyond its conscious choice."[12] All these dangers are in large measure present even today. A theology wholly bent on being academic and "scientific" according to the standards of the modern university, cuts itself off from its great historical matrices and renders itself sterile for the Church.

In this context, it is also necessary to consider how tensions can be constructively arbitrated. The fact that the Instruction rejects the appeal to the media as a channel of dialogue between the Magisterium and theology has encountered resolute opposition. It is comprehensible that the media themselves have reacted with exasperation to this passage, but it is obvious that theologians are equally reluctant to relinquish this weapon. Whereas the paper of the German-speaking Study Guild is worded rather prudently, the Austrian theologians declare quite bluntly that in the face of possible canonical measures whereby the Magisterium might attempt to "impose its

[11] Ibid., 272
[12] Ibid., 272f.

own line", "counterpressure by means of the mass media is un-avoidable." My intention is not to discuss at length the peculiar conception of the Magisterium, of pressure and counterpres-sure which the Austrian theologians set before us. Regarding the matter itself, it must be conceded that numbers 29 to 31 of the Instruction can be misunderstood if they are isolated from their context, especially paragraphs 25 and 26. Taken out of context, in fact, they can give rise to the impression that the Instruction allows the theologian the sole option of submitting divergent opinions to the magisterial authorities in secret and obliges him to suffer in silence if he is unsuccessful.[13] Never-theless, in the light of the whole text, which speaks of fruitful tensions and their value, it is quite obvious that the Instruction is not proposing "secret" communications but dialogue which remains on an ecclesiastical and scientific plane and avoids dis-tortions at the hands of the mass media. If this is "secret", then all science must be called "secret". In actuality, the point is precisely to use arguments instead of pressure as a means of persuasion. And when theologians reproach the Magisterium with mistrust (where do they detect it?), it is difficult to dismiss the suspicion that for their part they do not believe it possible to impress the Magisterium with reasoned arguments, so that the only choice left is to have recourse to power instead. Today it is very easy to mobilize the influence of the media against the Magisterium of the Church. I find it inconceivable that anyone can entertain the notion that truth and unity in the Church are to be served by these expedients. We may, in fact, legitimately assume that in such cases of loyal dissent there are issues at stake which presuppose knowledge of the science of theology and the believer's sympathy with the Church. Neither of these is the concern of the mass media, which in these circumstances cannot contribute any added depth to the dispute, though they

[13] The text is understood in this way by W. Groß, "Prophet gegen Institu-tion im alten Israel? Warnung vor vermeintlichen Gegensätzen", in: *Theolog. Quartalschr.* 171 (1991): 15–30; in addition to this, see 21, n. 19.

can indeed exacerbate conflicts. In modern society, which is dominated by the media, the law of the Church and the power of Rome, which are allegedly so perilous, appear, on the contrary, like the young David facing the giant Goliath. When the bearers of the apostolic office dare today to exercise the authority which has been committed to them in matters of doctrine, they enter almost inevitably into the form of apostolic existence depicted by Saint Paul: "[W]e have become, and are now, as the refuse of the world, the offscouring of all things" (1 Cor 4:13). The authority of the Church can continue to be exercised in our society only in the sign of contradiction, and precisely in this way it returns to its true nature.

c. Prophetic vs. episcopal tradition?

I would like to end by addressing one further observation to the text of Latin American—especially Brazilian—theologians, which has already been mentioned several times. To discuss its detailed accounts of historical matters and its vision of theology would surely exceed the limits of these reflections; doubtless, there are interesting points here which merit consideration. I wish to deal briefly with just one fundamental idea. Appealing to Ephesians 2:20 and referring to a formula of Cardinal Newman, the authors identify two streams of tradition, the episcopal and the prophetic, inasmuch as the Church is built upon the foundation of the apostles and prophets.[14] The two traditions are also apparently grounded in the confrontation and collaboration of the Apostles Peter and Paul, the first being the representative of conservation, the second of progress; the former the representative of the Judeo-Christian tradition, the latter the spokesman of the new Christianity coming from the Gentiles.[15] According to the text, this diversity is mirrored in corresponding differences of emphasis in Christology. Episcopal Christianity is said to privilege a juridical reading of the his-

---

[14] 774.
[15] Ibid., 777.

torical Jesus and the college of apostles, whereas the prophetic
tradition is supposedly based primarily on the risen and glo-
rified Christ, who through the Holy Spirit dwells in history,
especially in the oppressed and in their cry for life and freedom.
This tradition understands the Twelve essentially as a messianic
community and as the symbolic gathering of the New Israel
together with all the poor. Its characteristic is listening to the
Spirit-Christ, in the sense, for example, of John 16:13: "But
when the Spirit of truth comes, he will guide you into all
truth."[16]

It is no doubt correct that the Christian tradition admits of
different emphases and that it is necessary constantly to open
and broaden the seductive, but unilaterally juridical, conception of the Church as an institution by keeping our eyes on the
dimension of pneumatology. On the other hand, the distribu-
tion of these diverse forms onto two lines of tradition, the episcopal and the prophetic, is debatable. A thorough examination
of what the category of the prophetic does and does not mean is
urgently to be desired. W. Groß formulates the conclusion of a
painstaking investigation of the Old Testament evidence in the
following words: "However, even if it is limited to the writing
prophets from Amos to Ezekiel, there is simply no truth in the
widespread conception that within a people of Yahweh which
is in principle functional, or at least capable of reform, the task
of safeguarding the necessary tension between charism and office by means of radical critique devolves essentially upon the
prophets as antagonistic counterparts to the office holders."[17]
This permits Groß to observe that, "the prophetic as a total
category does not clarify but mystifies."[18] The stock clichés
customarily employed by the forces of protest to authenticate
themselves as the bearers of prophecy in contrast to the ministerial office are untenable. The whole biblical-ecclesial tradition

---

[16] Ibid., 781.
[17] Groß, 29.
[18] Ibid., 23.

must become the starting point of a new search beyond such vulgarizations for the true raison d'être and the genuine rights of prophecy. If it is permissible to inquire about the deepest essence of the prophetic despite the great diversity of guises in which it appears, we can probably locate it in the fact that the prophet has a direct mission from God and ultimately can appeal only to this immediate commission.[19] This also entails, of course—as W. Groß has shown—that prophecy can "be had only at the price of false prophecy".[20] In the end, it is never definitively clear except in retrospect who was an authentic prophet. There is no doubt that truly prophetic figures have also been given to the Church in every age, whether we think of Hildegard of Bingen, of Francis of Assisi, of Catherine of Siena, of Saint Brigid of Sweden or of Saint Ignatius of Loyola, to name just a few examples. Nor is there any doubt that the ministerial office of the Church is exposed to the risk of disregarding prophetic voices on account of their being uncomfortable. In consequence, we must all allow ourselves, in an attitude of vigilance, to be called into question again and again by such challenges and must remain open to the presence of the Spirit, who can be altogether uncomfortable. The discernment of spirits, such as the first Letter to the Thessalonians demands in response to the dubious prophets and prophecies of the time (5:9ff.), remains our permanent task. Both the acceptance of justified criticism and the protection of the faithful from falsifications of the Gospel, from an adulteration of the faith by the spirit of the world which passes itself off as the Holy Spirit, are integral parts of this discernment. We can learn it only in a deep interior union with Christ, in an obedience to the Word of God which finds ever-new expression in our lives and in an inner rooting in the living Church of all places and all times. But we are all in constant need of forgiveness and correction.

[19] Cf. ibid., 26.
[20] Ibid., 30.

Questions concerning Priestly Formation in Germany

Prefatory Note

In the spring of 1989, the German bishops, gathered under the presidency of the Holy Father, met in Rome with representatives of the individual curial offices in order to discuss in common the pastoral challenges of the present. I was commissioned to open the dialogue on issues of priestly formation. Thus, my task was to stimulate discussion and to formulate questions rather than to issue instructions or recipes. In so doing, I attempted to anchor the principal problems in a sketch of the situation whose development I myself have witnessed as a professor in Germany. In the meanwhile, the 1990 synod of bishops has dealt thoroughly with this theme; an outgrowth of the synod was the postsynodal apostolic exhortation *Pastores dabo vobis* (1992), which shapes the results of the synodal dialogues into concrete norms for action. In applying these norms to Germany, it is necessary to take into account the particular conditions of the German milieu such as they have evolved in the course of history. The fact that in Germany the Church-state relationship is governed by legal conditions which do not exist in other countries must not, however, serve as a justification for inactivity. On the contrary, it must lead to creative exertion aimed at bringing the impulses of the universal Church to bear in our situation. The questions which I formulated in 1989 continue, it seems to me, to be helpful for such an effort; their fundamental orientation was unequivocally confirmed by the synod. It is for this reason that what I said then is reprinted here. May it mark the transition from theory to the practice of the present hour.

1. Problems

Whoever wishes to comprehend how today's problems have arisen must first consider attentively a series of empirical developments in the ambit of institutions of Catholic theology in Germany,[1] developments which in the last thirty years have fundamentally transformed the landscape of theological endeavor.

The first such development was a considerable extension of professional theological teaching which had been underway since the beginning of the 1960s. A whole multitude of new theological faculties [*Fakultäten*][2] was born; individual chairs in the colleges of education [*Pädagogische Hochschulen*] were expanded into departments and equipped with academic privileges; additional institutions for the teaching of theology, which were not faculties in the strict sense, came into being, such as the theology divisions at the Universities of Saarbrücken, Frankfurt, Osnabrück and at the University of Paderborn, to name only a few examples. Correspondingly, the number of professorships grew by leaps and bounds, not only in the new or expanded institutions, but also in the already existing faculties. The formation of a new stratum of teachers, the so-called "academic middle corps" [*Akademischer Mittelbau*], proved to be of equal importance. On the one hand, the "middle corps" worked in greater proximity to the students and thus occasionally outstripped the professors in influence. On the other hand,

---

[1] Inasmuch as Cardinal Ratzinger was addressing an all-German audience, he could assume a familiarity with the German system of higher education. American readers, on the other hand, should keep in mind that for the most part German educational institutions have no exact counterparts in the United States. In order to enhance comprehension of the text, the translator has supplied the original German terms, sometimes accompanied by short explanatory notes, wherever it seemed opportune to do so [TRANS.].

[2] The *Fakultät* in the German university corresponds more or less to the "college" (e.g. "the college of engineering") in an American university [TRANS.].

it was less qualified technically and could hardly be tested on its spiritual aptitude. At first, the ranks of the professors could still count mostly on clerics to satisfy the rapidly increasing demand for teaching personnel, whereas in the "middle corps" the lay element was bound to become predominant very quickly. It is easy to foresee that this situation would be carried over into the professorate in the near future. Perhaps even more decisive than this transformation in the occupational profile of the teacher of theology was and is the circumstance that the pressure to meet more expeditiously the demand for teachers also altered the standard of qualification. It was inevitable that candidates, again especially in the "middle corps", were selected almost exclusively for considerations of a professional competence judged according to purely functional criteria. This phenomenon, in turn, is connected with a progressive narrowing into specialization. Whereas thirty years ago one was still required to master an oral examination cutting across the whole spectrum of theological specializations before being admitted to teach theology, in most exam regulations today three specializations suffice. Furthermore, these are usually understood to be a sort of sample study [*Exemplarisches Studium*] and are therefore very narrowly circumscribed in content. Add to this the fact that the notion of sample study often dominates even in university degree examinations [*Diplomprüfungen*],[3] and it becomes obvious how little is needed to obtain a doctorate or *habilitation*[4] in theology nowadays. One can become a doctor in theology without being familiar with the Greek Bible (to say nothing at all of the Hebrew), without being capable of reading medieval texts—just to illustrate aspects of the situation with a few "samples".

This specialization is the motor which keeps the single

[3] The *Diplom* is an official certification that one has completed the exams which are required for "graduation" from the university; it is approximately equivalent to the M.A. degree [TRANS.].

[4] In Germany, the *Habilitation* is an advanced degree—one stage beyond the doctorate—which used to be required for a university professorship [TRANS.].

branches of theology steadily drifting apart and thereby leads to a progressive obscuring of the unity of theology—which may also happen for the simple reason that such unity often does not really exist. This situation had been preceded in its own turn by an internal reshuffling of priorities in the theological faculties. Not only did the notion of the full equality of all the branches of theology bring about the disappearance of the intrinsic hierarchy of the disciplines; thanks principally to the far-reaching extension of so-called "practical theology", which in many places evolved into a faculty within the faculty, new standards of appraisal arose in its place. The special methodological character of "practical theology" quite often made the human sciences appear to be its real *prima philosophia*. Running a parallel course were the expulsion of exegesis out of the totality of theology into the realm of pure literature and the methodological dependence of moral theology on "practical theology", or better, upon the human sciences which furnished its guiding norms.

The augmentation of the teaching corps did not happen by accident: it was caused essentially by the vigorous swelling of the number of students. Whereas, at the beginning of the sixties, student enrollments even at large faculties usually still remained about three hundred, today the figure two thousand has in some places already been reached or even surpassed. Naturally, this triggered a change in the interior profile of the students. Candidates for the priesthood became the small minority; ordinary university students and various types of teacher training courses now predominated. The practice of teaching theology could not remain unaffected. Whereas theology had previously addressed the student fundamentally as a future priest, its spiritual orientation was bound to become ever more vague due to the impossibility of providing for every professional interest under a single umbrella. As a matter of course, it turned into a sort of pure instruction which constrained a certain academic neutrality designed to persuade by means of reason where nothing else could be presupposed with certainty.

Paradoxically, an additional trend toward growing publicity is connected with the tendency toward ever greater specialization. Theology is discovering its media and political power: a small but vociferous cadre of professors now employs it consciously as a means of influence in the Church.

Against this backdrop, it is easy to explain the reenforcement of a twofold movement toward autonomy from the Church's ministerial office and toward the intellectualization of theology, a movement which goes hand in hand with redoubled dependence on the state. An excessively rapid quantitative expansion of theology and a flattening of its spiritual profile help account for the cases, which have unfortunately become very frequent, of priest-professors who, because of their refusal of celibacy, have had to withdraw from theological faculties. These latter then become more and more distasteful to the state, which is obliged to support them financially, as well as to the universities, which must make room for these colleagues in other faculties where they are not really wanted and for which they also often lack the proper qualifications.

All of this must not mislead us into making blanket condemnations. Since I myself have taught in German faculties for more than twenty years and am still a member of a faculty of Catholic theology in that country, I set great store by the observation that now as ever there is a large corps of distinguished theologians who pursue their work in sober objectivity, with great scholarly competence and in a profound ecclesial disposition. But precisely those who know and emphasize this fact will feel it their duty not to pass over in silence the dangers and to look for ways to overcome them.

2. In Search of Answers

There is no ready-made recipe for surmounting the problems mentioned above. I have no solutions to offer but can only pose fresh questions in the hope of finding possible directions for the road ahead.

a. On the future development of the faculties and related institutions

It must first be observed that the new facilities, whose difficulties I have alluded to, were not brought into existence by chance. The widening scope of professional practice, and in particular the increasing demands for instruction, produced the new institutions and positions. Insofar as these demands also continue to exist in reality and must be acknowledged as necessities in the light of an honest analysis of the actual need, we must accept the new facilities which have been created so far. The first question, then, would be to what extent the demands to which the new institutions responded can still be considered essential. Since, in the present situation, it is certainly not possible to speak of a surplus of candidates for the priesthood, such an analysis would have to bear on the range of pastoral ministries requiring university-level qualifications and on the field of religious education. I cannot attempt this analysis, but, even independently of it, it is possible to make a few points:

1. Even if all of the demands in their existing volume were recognized to be indispensable, one must admit that there are superfluous facilities which are not absolutely necessary. The reduction of positions is quite feasible and, as the most recent consolidations in the state's jurisdiction have shown, it is even possible to make do without entire institutions.

2. In any case, on the whole the number of students remains higher than the number of actual demands to be met in the Church. It is almost inevitable that quite soon there is going to be a considerable body of unemployed theologians. It seems to me, therefore, that responsibility—at the very least—toward young people urgently requires a *numerus clausus* calculated according to current job opportunities. This policy would in its

turn have repercussions on the range of positions which are truly necessary.

3. Cut-backs are entirely possible in the "middle corps" as well. Above all, however, requirements of an academic and ecclesial nature should be more rigorously defined in order to facilitate a better selection.

4. The tendency to specialize narrowly in advancement to academic degrees should be reversed in favor of a broad-based approach, so that theology as a unified whole constitutes the foundation of the degree. Moreover, in teaching appointments more attention should be paid to the capacity to teach theology from the organic perspective of the whole and to pursue it in conformity with its essence as a scientific reflection on the faith of the Church. The episcopal *nihil obstat* should not sink to the level of an empty formality simply bestowed in advance by an authority extraneous to the university. It must rather be administered with great responsibility, as playing a part in shaping from within the *modus operandi* of theology.

5. The question of the actual and, from the point of view of the nature and mission of the Church, reasonable demand for pastoral assistants with an academic degree calls for the same searching investigation as does the question concerning the nature, scope and function of religious education.

2. The significance of the seminary

Paradoxically, at the very moment when theological faculties and related institutes have been experiencing a growth boom, the seminaries have suffered a massive loss in function, while, incidentally, the colleges affiliated with religious orders [*Ordenshochschulen*] have disappeared on a large scale (a matter which we need not consider here). Up until the second half of the 1960s, the seminaries in many parts of Germany also undertook a number of offices which supplemented the teaching of theology, and this chiefly in two ways. First, through the institution of "coaches" [*Repetenten*], which since then has generally been supplanted by the "academic middle corps". As a state institution, however, the "middle corps" can only partially exercise the role of the seminary coaches, who in close personal contact with the students had assisted them in assimilating the academic material in an individual, even spiritual fashion. Second, the seminaries, depending on the region, offered theological instruction programs at the end of university studies. Taking the form of a two- to three- or four-semester course, these programs were of a predominantly, though not exclusively, practical character. They complemented academic formation and oriented it to pastoral work. Both have disappeared, except for small vestiges. In most German dioceses, the seminary years are almost completely filled with practicums and hardly still leave room for teaching. This means that an important opportunity for spiritual and ecclesial deepening of academic instruction slips away precisely at a time when such instruction is less and less able to relate to priestly life and spirituality, considering the many-layered diversity of the student body.

To my mind, the fashioning of seminaries into centers where students receive a qualitatively excellent spiritual formation while deepening theological instruction imparted in the classroom is a paramount task of the present hour and a significant chance to offset the problems of the faculties, which are at the moment insoluble. By the same token, the question of a propaedeutic year prior to beginning academic study, of whose necessity I am personally more and more convinced, should also be seriously examined. The bipolarity of the seminary and the faculty belongs to the specific character of the German tradition in priestly formation. Precisely if we wish to retain the faculties as essential partners in this formation, it is important to restore this bipolar situation and to avoid falling prey to a claim of totality on the part of the academy which reduces the seminary to a mere lodging. It seems to me that quite concrete possibilities are opening up in this direction; let us hasten to make them a reality.

Acknowledgments

Faith, Philosophy and Theology. Address delivered upon the receipt of the degree of doctor *honoris causa* in humane letters from the College of Saint Thomas in St. Paul, Minnesota, 1984; repeated on October 22, 1984, to mark the four hundredth jubilee of the seminary and theological faculty of Fulda; published in: *Internationale katholische Zeitschrift Communio* 14 (1985): 56–66;

    English: "Faith, Philosophy and Theology", in: ICaR 11 (1984): 350–63; Pope John Paul II Lecture Series, College of St. Thomas (1985), 10–14 [the text has been entirely retranslated from the German for the purposes of the present book —Trans.];

    French: "Foi, théologie et philosophie", in: *Communio* 10 (1985): 24–37; and in: J. Ratzinger, *Église et théologie* (Paris, 1992), 15–36.

On the Essence of the Academy and Its Freedom. A considerably abbreviated and reworked version of the lecture given in Munich on June 27, 1982, to commemorate the twenty-fifth anniversary of the Catholic Academy of Bavaria; published under the title: "Interpretation—Kontemplation—Aktion: Überlegungen zum Auftrag einer katholischen Akademie", in: *Internationale katholische Zeitschrift Communio* 12 (1983): 167–79; as well as in: *Église et théologie*, 37–64.

The Spiritual Basis and Ecclesial Identity of Theology. Given as the "President's lecture" at St. Michael's College, Toronto (April 4, 1986); presented in Italian in Brescia (March 22, 1986) and in Bologna (April 30, 1986); published under the title "Theologie und Kirche", in: *Internationale katholische Zeitschrift Communio* 15 (1986): 515–33;

    English: The Church as an Essential Dimension of Theology (University of St. Michael's College), Toronto, 1986 (offprint) [the piece has been newly translated from the German for this book—TRANS.];

Italian: "Teologia e Chiesa", in: *Communio* 15, no. 87 (1986): 92–111;

French: "Église et théologie", 93–129.

Pluralism as a Problem for Church and Theology. Published in: *Forum katholische Theologie* 2 (1986): 81–96;

Italian: "Unità e pluralismo nella Chiesa dal Concilio al post-Concilio", in: *Bolletino diocesano per gli ufficiali e attività pastorali dell'arcidiocesi di Bari* 61, no. 1 (1985); *Orientamenti pastorali* 12 (1985): 125–44.

On the "Instruction concerning the Ecclesial Vocation of the Theologian". Part 2: hitherto unpublished; Part 1: published in: *Internationale katholische Zeitschrift Communio* 19 (1990): 561–65.

Questions concerning Priestly Formation in Germany. Hitherto unpublished.